The Strategist CEO

Recent Titles from Quorum Books

The Strategist CEO

HOW VISIONARY EXECUTIVES BUILD ORGANIZATIONS

MICHEL ROBERT

QUORUM BOOKS

NEW YORK · WESTPORT, CONNECTICUT · LONDON

Library of Congress Cataloging-in-Publication Data

Robert, Michel.
  The strategist CEO.

  Includes index.
    1. Strategic planning.   2. Organizational effective-
ness.   3. Chief executive officers.   I. Title.
HD30.28.R63   1988   658.4'012   87-10945
ISBN 0-89930-268-8 (lib. bdg. : alk. paper)

British Library Cataloguing in Publication Data is available.

Copyright © 1988 by Michel Robert

Library of Congress Catalog Card Number: 87-10945
ISBN: 0-89930-268-8

First published in 1988 by Quorum Books

Greenwood Press, Inc.
88 Post Road West, Westport, Connecticut 06881

Printed in the United States of America

The paper used in this book complies with the
Permanent Paper Standard issued by the National
Information Standards Organization (Z39.48-1984).

10 9 8 7 6 5 4 3 2 1

Copyright Acknowledgments

The author and publisher gratefully acknowledge permission to reproduce
excerpts from the following copyrighted materials:

Quotations reprinted from various issues of *Business Week*. © 1981–1986
by McGraw-Hill, Inc.

Walter Kiechel III, *Fortune*, © 1982 Time Inc. All rights reserved.

Michael Porter, "The State of Strategic Thinking," *The Economist*, May 23, 1987.

Bill Saporito, *Fortune*, © 1984 Time Inc. All rights reserved.

Lee Smith, *Fortune*, © 1981 Time Inc. All rights reserved.

Contents

Preface

This book is for people who run organizations. It contains ideas and concepts which are of the utmost importance to such people—*how* to develop a strategy and chart the *direction* of an organization, and involve its key executives in an *orderly process* in order to obtain their commitment so that the strategy is implemented successfully.

In view of the explosion of literature on this subject in recent years, a few words might be in order about what this book is and and what it is not.

First, it is not theory. It is not crammed with charts, surveys, statistics, or questionnaires. Such is not the basis upon which we found strategy and direction being set in well-managed organizations. *People* run organizations—not studies.

This book has two unique features. First, it describes a *unique* process of setting and implementing strategy. This book is not about a *planning system* which utilizes elaborate matrices, bar graphs, flow charts with lines, bubbles, and squares all presented in kaleidoscopic fashion. Rather, it is a reflection of the *thought process* which we saw successful CEOs use to develop a coherent strategy to deal with the environment the business faces. It is a pragmatic, time-efficient tool or "framework" which enables management to clarify and articulate the *strategic vision* they wish to pursue.

Second, it was developed while working *with* CEOs and their senior executives in a number of organizations. Some of these organizations are well-known corporations such as 3M, Honeywell, Volvo, Supervalu, Fiat, Newmont Mining, and some mid-size and fast growing ones such as FLEX-con, *Working Woman* magazine, and Health Dimensions. Altogether, we have worked with some 130 companies of all sizes and in many countries. Confidentiality agreements with our clients do not permit us to divulge the exact outcome of the work done with them. As a result we have not associated any examples with specific clients. When organizations are named, we have done so because their actions are general knowledge and anyone could come to the same conclusions we have.

This book is also not for losers. Our clients are among some of the most progressive and best managed organizations that exist. This has caused us to note one important trait about successful people running successful organizations—their continuous willingness to learn and improve.

Finally, this book has been designed to be a "quick read." We have included enough examples to illustrate key ideas while attempting to restrict the number of examples used so not to burden the reader with unnecessary minutiae.

> Good reading!
> —*Michel Robert*

Acknowledgments

This book could not have been written without the cooperation of all Decision Processes International (DPI) partners and their clients. I wish to thank all my colleagues and their clients who volunteered time and effort to challenge, debate, and eventually shape the ideas presented in this document.

ONE

Why CEOs Have Difficulty Implementing Their Strategy

"My job," says Ken Olsen, CEO of Digital Equipment Corporation, "is to make sure we have a strategy and everyone follows it." This is a simple, yet powerful, job description for every CEO. Getting "everyone to follow" the strategy, however, is easier said than done. Many CEOs we have met over the years have not encountered the same success as Ken Olsen. In fact, over the course of several years, we have frequently heard the statement, "It's easy to develop a strategy, it's the *implementation* that's difficult." Our own experience shows that the *formulation* of a strategy is as difficult as its implementation. There are, however, several reasons that many CEOs have difficulty getting people to implement their strategy.

THE STRATEGY IS IMPLICIT AND NOT EXPLICIT

In too many organizations, the strategy of the company is implicit and resides in the head of the chief executive solely. Most chief executives have a strategy. However, they have great difficulty articulating it to people around them.

One senior executive of a Fortune 500 company once said to us, "the reason I have difficulty implementing my CEO's strategy is because I don't know what it is!"

Lesson No. 1: People cannot implement what they don't know

Because CEOs have difficulty verbalizing their strategy, most people are placed in the position of having to "guess" what the strategy is, and they may guess wrong. Or else, they learn what the strategy is over time by the nature of the decisions they recommend which are accepted or rejected. Gradually, a subordinate learns where the line of demarcation is between the things that are permitted by the strategy and those that are not. This is called "strategy by groping" because the strategy becomes clear or explicit only over a long period of time during which people may have spent too much time pursuing and implementing activities that did not fit while not paying enough attention to opportunities that represented a better strategic fit.

THE STRATEGY IS DEVELOPED IN ISOLATION

A second reason why the strategy may not be implemented properly is that it was developed by the CEO in isolation. Many CEOs have a strategy but their key people are not involved in the *process* and therefore have no ownership. In such a case, subordinates usually do not understand the rationale behind the strategy and will spend more time questioning it than implementing it. The CEO becomes more and more impatient as subordinates question his logic more and more deeply. The CEO, on the other hand, can't comprehend why his people are not executing what, to him, is a simple strategy.

Lesson No. 2: People don't implement properly what they don't understand!

Some CEOs might involve one or two people in the formulation of the strategy. This is better than doing it alone but is still not good enough. The *entire* management team must be involved in order to achieve accurate understanding and proper execution.

As Dale Lang, chairman of *Working Woman* and *McCall's* magazines, noted as a reason for using our strategic process, "I could have dictated to the staff what I wanted to do, but it's a whole lot better if they reach the conclusion themselves. In that way, they're working their plan and know how and why they chose it."

THE STRATEGY IS DEVELOPED BY AN OUTSIDE CONSULTANT

This is the worst of all strategic crimes and the "kiss of death" for any strategy—even a good one. No outside consultant has the right to set the direction of your organization or knows as much as your own people about the business and the environment it is facing. Most strategies developed by outside consultants end up in the wastepaper basket for two reasons:

- everyone can quickly tear the conclusions apart because they are not based on an intimate knowledge of the company, the business, or the industry.
- there is no commitment to that strategy by senior management because it is not *their* strategy.

Experience has shown that almost any strategy will work, unless it is completely invalidated by negative environmental factors. Experience has also shown, however, that *no* strategy will work if a couple or a few members of senior management are not committed to that strategy. In effect, if total commitment is not present, those uncommitted to the strategy will, on a day-to-day basis, do everything in their power to prove it wrong. We suspect that James Dutt's troubles in implementing his vision and strategy at Beatrice Food stemmed from this difficulty.

Lesson No. 3: People don't implement what they are not committed to

In order to obtain commitment, key managers must be involved at each step of the process so that their views are heard and discussed. Participation, although sometimes time-consuming, breeds commitment. Key managers buy into the strategy because they helped construct it. It is as much *their* strategy as the CEO's.

Many CEOs have used our process knowing in advance the outcome. They did so anyway, using it as a tool to tap the advice and knowledge of their people and to obtain commitment to the conclusion so that implementation of the strategy can then proceed expeditiously. The Japanese call this "nima washi"—bottom-up commitment.

THE CRITICAL ISSUES ARE NOT IDENTIFIED

One aspect of strategy is its formulation, another is thinking through its implications. Most strategic planning systems we have seen used in organizations don't encourage people to think through the implications of their strategy. As a result, they end up reacting to these events as they are encountered and many people start losing faith in the strategy. "There were so many holes in the CEO's strategy, I gave up trying to implement it," is how a sector vice-president of a major organization put it. Every strategy, especially if it represents a change of direction, has implications.

Lesson No. 4: People give up on a strategy whose implications have not been anticipated

A good strategic process should help management identify and proactively manage the implications of a strategy on the company's products, markets, customers, organization structure, personnel, and culture.

OPERATIONAL PEOPLE ARE NOT GOOD STRATEGIC THINKERS

The above statement is true because most people spend their entire careers with an organization dealing exclusively with operational issues. With few exceptions, we have found that only the CEO or the general manager sees the "big picture" and views the business and its environment in strategic terms There usually is only one strategist in any organization and that is the CEO. Most managers are so engrossed in operational activity that they have not developed the skill of thinking strategically. Therefore, they have difficulty coping with strategic issues, especially if these are "sprung" on them out-of-the-blue. "The problem," says Milton Lauenstein in an article in the *Journal of Business Strategy*, "is that many executives have only the fuzziest notion of the functions of strategy formulation."

Lesson No. 5: The CEO may encourage the participation of key subordinates in the strategic process for strictly educational value

People will implement a strategy more effectively if they understand the difference between a strategic process and either long-range or operational planning together with the difference between strategic and operational issues.

The fact that *two-thirds* of the companies on *Fortune*'s original 1955 list are no longer on it only thirty-one years later and that *one-third* of those on the list in 1970 are also no longer there only seventeen years later says a lot about the *strategic thinking* ability of American executives. And all this has occurred during the emergence of so-called *strategic planning systems* that have enamoured business executives for the last fifteen years!

One element that has contributed significantly to the lack of strategic skills in many executives has been the emergence, during the 1970s and early 1980s, of strategic planning systems that are highly *quantitative* in nature and not *qualitative*. These so-called planning systems are really long-range operational systems that force managers into linear extrapolations of the "numbers" into the future without affecting the direction or composition of the business.

Organizations that embarked on these time-consuming planning systems imposed them on management, insisting at the same time that these "strategic plans" be addressed every twelve months. Because of the "fire drill" orientation of strategic planning systems, strategic *thinking* in many major organizations came to a standstill. *There simple wasn't time to think strategically*. These systems have been a major cause of the loss of American competitiveness during the last decade. As a senior executive of one of America's best-managed companies, according to *Fortune* magazine and Tom Peters of *In Search of Excellence*, said to us, "Our corporate planning system is more interested in the *form* than the *process*." Amen!

WHAT IS THE STRATEGIC QUOTIENT OF YOUR ORGANIZATION?

If you are interested at this point in assessing your organization's strategic skill, you may wish to answer the following questions and have your direct reports do the same.

1. Do you have a well-articulated, clear statement of strategy and business concept?

   Yes ☐   No ☐

2. Could you write a one- or two-sentence statement of that strategy?

   Yes ☐   No ☐

3. Do your key subordinates understand that strategy?

   Yes ☐   Somewhat ☐   No ☐

4. Could each of your subordinates write a one- or two-sentence statement of that strategy without consulting you or each other?

One Person Could ☐   Some Could ☐   None Could ☐

5. Do they use this statement as a guide for the choices they make in pursuing products, markets, and customers?

Use Frequently ☐   Use Sometimes ☐   Never Use ☐

6. Is it effective in helping you to choose or reject products, markets, and customers?

Very Effective ☐   Somewhat Effective ☐   Not Effective ☐

7. Have you ever sat down as a management team to try to obtain consensus as to the future direction of your firm?

   Yes ☐   No ☐

8. Was consensus obtained or are there still different visions of what the organization is trying to become?

Total Consensus   Some Consensus   Little Consensus
(Single Vision) ☐   (Fuzzy Vision) ☐   (Different Visions)☐

9. Is the organization moving in a clear direction?

   Yes ☐   Not Sure ☐   No ☐

10. Do you have a separate process of strategic thinking to determine *what* you want to become as opposed to *how* you get there?

    Yes ☐   No ☐

11. What is your business concept?

_____

_____

_____

If all the answers are similar and each person's definition of your business concept is identical, then you are in good shape. The wider the discrepancies in their replies compared to yours, the less clear is your strategy and you may wish to read the following few chapters.

TWO

Strategic Planning: The Death Knell of Strategic Thinking

People run organizations—studies do not. Yet despite this simple truth, major corporations in recent years have relied on "strategic" planning techniques for setting company direction. These unwieldy, complex systems are based on *quantitative* analyses of markets and competition.

While initially perceived by top management as magic formulas for success, these same planning systems are now spurned by management and have proved to be an obstacle to sound business strategy. Organizations run by systems have been known to misjudge the marketplace or acquire companies unrelated to their own business concept. The result has been misallocation of resources and substantial financial loss.

Rather than a reliance on one or another of several modern management techniques, it is a clear, concise business concept that is central to the success of an organization. The key and missing link to this brand of management is clear *strategic thinking*.

Even Michael Porter of the Harvard Business School had this to say about strategic planning in a recent interview with the *Economist*:

Strategic planning in most companies has not contributed to strategic thinking. The need for strategic thinking has never been greater.... The processes for strategic planning were not promoting strategic thinking. My own view is that strategic thinking is the glue that holds together the many systems and initiatives within a company.

Currently, strategic thinking is a lost skill in the American business community. There are a number of reasons for this shortcoming.

A NUMBERS APPROACH TO FORWARD PLANNING

The foundation of these planning systems is mostly internally generated data which is highly *quantitative* and historical in nature.

Most long-range planning systems look back at five years of history— the numbers—and extrapolate forward for the next five years. This kind of planning does nothing to change the "look" or the composition of a business in terms of products, markets, and customers. It also assumes that outside influences will remain the same, in terms of competition, government, labor, resource availability, demographics, and perceptions, as well as other trends.

Most strategic planning systems we have seen used in corporations are really operational in nature. As such, they fail to take the whole picture into account. These systems are usually accompanied by a need to do a lot of analysis, usually requiring graphs, forms, bar charts, matrices, and volumes of numbers. Many of these systems also projected or expected past rates of growth to repeat themselves in the future. In such a scenario, one can be successful strictly by operational prowess.

Success, based on growth and operational effectiveness, is threatened or reduced in a period of mixed patterns of growth and only then does management start thinking strategically. It is in such times that resources become scarce and the need to allocate these resources more carefully surfaces.

PORTFOLIO MANAGEMENT WAS CONCEPTUALLY FLAWED

In the early 1970s, American business became enamoured of the "portfolio" approach to business strategy. This long-range planning approach, or system, was based on a market share/market growth matrix which classified businesses into "cash cows," "dogs," "stars," and so forth. This approach relied on the concept that to be the most profitable, a corporation had to have the largest market share.

Companies invested heavily in programs to increase their market shares, only to find themselves, in some instances, to have the largest share of their markets, yet to be the least profitable among their competitors.

On the other hand, a number of other companies with minuscule shares, but a very clear business concept, were sometimes found to be the most profitable. At the beginning of the 1980s, for this and other complex reasons, many organizations, at tremendous cost, found the matrix approach to be counterproductive and conceptually flawed.

A growth rate which fluctuates greatly from industry to industry, such as North America is currently experiencing, explains why the famous matrix of market share and market growth upon which the Boston Consulting Group built its reputation during the 70s has lost its glamour. In a recent article, *Business Week* ("The New Breed of Strategic Planner") drew the following conclusions on the subject of forward planning:

Companies can no longer depend on the old strategy of growth for growth's sake as a guarantee of success.

Indeed, even within the venerable hallways of the Boston Consulting Group which is usually credited with developing the product portfolio matrix on which so much planning of the 1970's was based, the portfolio concept has lost its luster.

The relationship between relative market share and profitability does not hold anymore.

Nowadays the question management must ask itself is twofold: How many businesses can we afford to be in without spreading ourselves too thin and what particular strengths do we as a company have that will enable us to survive in those businesses?

Fortune magazine has also endorsed these doubts about the market share-market growth matrix in an article by Walter Kiechel III, "Corporate Strategists Under Fire."

Having your business segmented into SBU's didn't tell you what to do with them. The experience curve proved useful mostly for products sold on the basis of price alone. How many industries really fit that commodity pattern?

What if you charted your business on a growth-share matrix and found you had only cows and dogs? The grid couldn't tell where your new businesses should come from.

The work being done at the corporate level arises from the widespread conclusion that a stack of notebooks, each containing an SBU strategy, together with a growth-share matrix of all the company's businesses, by themselves don't make up a corporate strategy. How can these help in figuring out what new businesses you should enter?

McKinsey, in an issue of its quarterly magazine, observed that "American business, it often seems, has done more *strategic planning* than *strategic thinking* in recent years."

A senior planning officer with the Mead Corporation concurs.

Market share–market growth strategy helped us a lot in the 1970's. Now everybody and his brother is in the game, and a grim period of disinflation has revealed severe cost problems in every corner of the matrix. If we used the same ideas in the 1980's, they would take the company right off the cliff.

William C. Waddell, in his book *The Outline of Strategy*, stated,

Tools or models are never a substitute for thinking. Critics of portfolio planning tools have assumed that giving a subsidiary a classification or assigning it a position on a grid *automatically determines the strategy that it is to follow*—a nonsensical procedure which would eliminate the need for thought.

Richard Hamermesh, in his book *Making Strategy Happen*, which is a study of the effects of the portfolio approach, stated, "The case of business strategy decisions, choices made solely on the basis of an SBU's position on a portfolio matrix can be very inappropriate." In the same book, Jim Ferguson of General Foods concluded, "In retrospect, the concept of cash cow and mature business got in the way of both growth and innovation." He cites the examples of coffee and instant puddings, two mature businesses, where opportunities to grow these businesses were lost because they had been identified as "cash cows."

Even Harold Geneen, who is credited with building ITT into a multidivisional powerhouse in the 60s and 70s, quickly saw the flaws of the portfolio approach to strategy: "I could not accept it. Not only would such a formula not work, it would violate everything we had built in 20 years at ITT. . . . Who would want to work for a company or a division labeled 'cash cow' whose earnings were ladled out to someone else and with no hope of future growth? Instinct tells me that a sound, money-making division with obviously good management should be encouraged and expanded, not milked for the benefit of a so-called 'star' whose ascendency is not ordained in the heavens."

Our own work with corporations large, medium, and small would confirm these conclusions. We have noticed too many exceptions to the market share equals profitability rule. There are many companies whose share is not dominant but yet continue to produce healthy profits year after year. In the automobile industry, we find Daimler-Benz, BMW, and Volvo. In the oil industry, we find Petrofina on an international level and literally hundreds of others on a national level. In the watch industry, we find Rolex of Switzerland still doing well in spite of the dominance of Japanese companies. In the data processing industry, we find Hewlett Packard and Digital in spite of IBM's dominant share. In the telecommunications industry we find Rolm and Northern Telecom in spite of AT&T's quasi-monopoly.

Another observation was that a dominant market share does not automatically bring with it profitability. General Motors dominates the U.S. automobile market yet it lost hundreds of millions in the late 1970s and in

1986 it was the least profitable company, on a per car basis, even with over 40% of the market. Amtrak is another example.

Because of reasons such as those elaborated above, the *Business Week* article "New Breed" also noted, "Even in a slow-growth industry, a company can stay vibrant." The people at General Foods demonstrated this by dropping the "cash cow" concept and introducing a new range of products containing aspartame. "Managing in the mature industries of the 1980's requires a new breed of executive. In short, a totally new type of Strategic Planning, conceived and implemented by a new type of executive is required."

Again, we would concur with part of the above statements. The executives may not necessarily need to be replaced but certainly their approach to setting direction *must* change. Our own key conclusion: *these planning techniques will not work in the 80s and 90s.*

It seems to us that the planning tools of the 60s and 70s were too heavily focused on the back-end of the business—market share—which is the *result* of a strategy and not *the* strategy. The market share/market growth portfolio approach is a good analytical tool to assess one's competitive position in the marketplace but it is not sufficient to base one's forward planning on that analysis exclusively. The portfolio approach is a two dimensional—share and growth—view of an organization while charting the future direction of an organization requires study and consideration of several additional elements. The portfolio approach is a tool to assist in the management of current products, but it provides little assistance for future products. Masaru Ibuka, co-founder of Sony, certainly did not have market share, market growth, or any competitors in mind when he conceived the idea of a portable tape deck. The Walkman was born because of Ibuka's interest in classical music and his desire to be able to listen to his favorite artists whenever he wished and not only at times when he would have access to the traditional immobile record player or tape deck. At the time, Sony's planners and market research people advised Ibuka and Akio Morita, Sony's other co-founder, to abandon the idea since they saw no market for a portable tape deck. In spite of this advice, they pushed ahead because they still thought that they were on to a good idea. And a good idea it proved to be. In three years, Sony sold over 4,000,000 Walkman sets. A similar story could be told about the home video recorder—the VCR—which is quickly revolutionizing the entertainment industry.

The portfolio analysis method ends up with conclusions as to whether the organization should harvest, defend, divest, or invest in various product lines. Our suggestion is that these conclusions must be filtered through another key question, which is: In *pursuit of which business concept, or strategy, are we harvesting, defending, divesting or investing?* In other words, such decisions have to be made within a higher level *strategic context* or framework.

THINKING MUST PRECEDE PLANNING

Forward planning, in our opinion, must start at the front-end of the business by defining the *business concept* or "raison d'être" of an organization. With a clearly defined and articulated business concept, an organization can prosper in a period of slow growth and increasing environmental uncertainty. The key to success is to periodically revisit the business concept to insure its validity in view of the environment that management is expecting the organization to cope with.

Examples of clear business concepts abound. Since its inception over one hundred years ago, Daimler-Benz has been pursuing one business concept only—"the best engineered car in the world." This singularity of purpose has enabled that company to prosper in good or bad times. With the automobile giants struggling with each other to survive, Daimler-Benz still has an eight month backlog of orders. Volvo's concept of "durability [16-year car] and safety" has helped that company to register record profits in spite of a small share.

The Rolex Company positions its products as "jewelry . . . not watches." As a result, it has survived the Japanese onslaught on the Swiss watch industry. More interesting, its best market is Japan, where most status-conscious Japanese prefer being seen wearing a Rolex rather than a Seiko.

Ford Europe, which was the cash engine and saviour of the Ford Motor Company in the late 1970s and early 1980s, has brought in billions of dollars with the concept of a "world car"—the Escort.

Other examples are Apple with its concept of a "personal computer," Federal Express with "guaranteed overnight delivery of letters and small parcels," and Johnson & Johnson which markets products only for "mothers, nurses, doctors, and patients."

There is strong evidence that family-owned companies continue to stay profitable because of the continuity of vision from one generation of family managers to another rather than any knowledge of modern management techniques.

A clear, concise business concept is the starting point and is imperative to the success of any organization. The key, and missing link, to this brand of management is *clear strategic thinking*.

THREE

Competitive Strategy: Going Forward ... Backwards!

In the last ten to fifteen years, American multi-nationals have lost large parcels of strategic ground to Japanese and German companies. Why has this occurred and why is it still occurring? Corporate America has never been as engrossed in techniques and formulas of competitive analysis and strategy as in the last decade and a half. First, there was the portfolio matrix approach based on the market share/market growth concept and in the last few years has emerged the value-chain concept. Yet America's competitive position worsens.

Both of these approaches to corporate strategy are flawed, and for the same reason. Their whole thrust is based on the underlying assumption that corporate strategy *starts* with an analysis of competitive position. That is a very myopic view of strategy. Furthermore, a strategy developed entirely on competitive analysis will always be, by its very nature, a *reactive* strategy and not a proactive one. And that is why most American businesses have been losing ground for the last fifteen years.

Akio Morita, co-founder of Sony, certainly did not have any competitive data when the decision to introduce the VCR or the Walkman was made. None existed. In fact, strategy based on competitive analysis may only make the organization overlook other lucrative opportunities outside its *existing* competitive arena. If Sony had limited its strategy to looking only at the competitors it had in the arena of transistor radios, its first product, it would never had developed the VCR or the Walkman. Obviously, a much much broader strategy, based on other factors than its current competitors, was at work in Morita's mind. Mr. Morita, in his recent book, articulated what has been Sony's business concept since its inception: "Masaru Ibuku (co-founder) and I had often spoken of the concept of our new company as an innovator, a clever company that would make new, high-technology products in ingenious ways."

Over the last few years, we have worked with the chief executives of some 130 corporations worldwide, both large and small, trying to codify the thought process that a CEO and the management team use to formulate a coherent and successful strategy. That work has shown us, over and over, that competition is indeed a variable in the strategic process but that it *is not* the first variable to consider, nor is it the most important. During our work with these CEOs, competition was almost never their major preoccupation. In fact, most of them were more concerned with competitors they did not yet have, than with their current competitors.

WHO'S THE COMPETITION?

Another difficulty in trying to develop a strategy by starting with an analysis of the competition is trying to determine who the competitors are. Competition *used* to be United versus American Airlines, each offering the same, regulated fares. Or Macy's versus Gimbel's. Or Ford and Chevy. Or Coke and Pepsi. Today, competition is exacerbated by technology, government intervention or lack of intervention, lifestyles, perceptions, growth, changing industry structure, new knowledge, demographics, and a host of other variables. United and American now compete in an unregulated environment against other, low-cost carriers, in a time when many buying decisions are made on the basis of frequent flyer bonus points. Gimbel's is gone, and Macy's competes against everything from other large chains, to K-Mart and Bloomingdale's, to small boutiques offering personalized service, to the local drug store down the block which has become a mini-department store. Competition, because of change, is becoming more difficult, harder to anticipate, harder to track, harder to understand, and much harder to combat. Competition no longer means simply your traditional competitors. It now means anything—anyone, any organization, any movement—that takes your customers' money away from you. So, movie theaters now compete against home video rental centers and cable TV; the post office now competes against Federal Express, and both compete against electronic mail; your bank competes against Merrill Lynch and Sears Roebuck, all of them offering a variety of competing financial services; Greyhound and Trailway buses now compete against airlines, of all things, offering no-frills fares, and both compete against Amtrak; board games compete against video games and computer games; mail-order catalogs compete against home television shopping; travel agents compete against direct, desk-top computer reservations systems.

Trying to determine who one's competitors are is sometimes akin to trying to find out "Who's on first?" As the CEO of a major company told us recently: "Our major competitor is also our largest supplier as well as our most important customer."

Today, one has to view competition in terms of alternative ways for the consumer to obtain the *results* desired, not as specific companies within your industry trying to underprice or outperform you. While the latter competition will always exist, it is just one component of the overall competitive picture.

If looking at the competitors is not the first step of setting strategy, what is the first step, and how does a CEO go about developing and implementing a successful strategy?

DETERMINE THE ORGANIZATION'S STRATEGIC ANCHOR

The first step in the strategic process is for the CEO and the management team to identify and agree on which element of the business is strategically more important to them and around which they can leverage the business in order to develop strategic advantage. In other words, what part of the business is at the root of the company's successful products, markets, and customers and represents the company's strategic weapon? More will be said on this element of strategy in chapter 6 entitled "The Heart of Strategic Thinking: The Driving Force."

EVALUATE THE ENVIRONMENT

The second element we observed was an assessment of the *qualitative* variables, internally but primarily externally, that might work for or against the organization in the future. These variables are usually locked inside the heads of the people running the business and must be extracted and debated in a structured and objective forum with an outside person facilitating the process.

DEVELOP A COHERENT STRATEGY AND VISION

No company can pursue two strategies simultaneously, since usually no company has the resources to do so. It becomes imperative for management to agree to *one* strategy that best positions the organization vis-à-vis the environment it faces. The strategy needs to be articulated in a short but succinct paragraph or less, so that it can be clearly communicated to the dozens, hundreds, or thousands of people who will be counted upon to carry it out. This strategy statement represents the *conceptual underpinning* of the business and the organizations' "raison d'être." The strategy then needs to be translated into a "vision" or profile outlining clearly what the organization will look like in the future.

ANTICIPATE THE IMPLICATIONS OF YOUR STRATEGY

The next step is to anticipate the implications of that strategy and identify the critical issues management must address itself to in order for the strategy to work. We have often seen a well-conceived and potentially viable strategy fail because the implications of that strategy had been ignored. Anticipating and managing these implications proactively is the only way to assure the success of any strategy. Then comes the competition segment.

CHOOSE YOUR COMPETITORS, DO NOT LET YOUR COMPETITORS CHOOSE YOU

A proactive strategy, together with a good strategic process, will then allow the management team to identify which competitors the strategy might attract. This next concept is crucial to any successful strategy—*choose the competitors you wish to compete successfully against.* No company has the resources to compete with all competitors, nor does it need to do so. Equip yourself to compete with the competitors you choose by knowing their strengths and weaknesses. Another fallacy of competitive schooling is the concept of attacking their weaknesses. This approach will only cause the competitor to shore-up that area and will make the competitor stronger. If you want your strategy to work against *certain* competitors, attack and neutralize their *strengths*! A little more costly perhaps in the short-term, but a lot more successful in the long-term. Chapter 11, "Using Strategic Thinking for Competitive Advantage," will describe ways on how to use this process as a competitive tool.

CONTROL THE "SANDBOX"

The mark of a successful strategy is that it allows you to control, or at least influence, the terms of play in the "competitive sandbox." If you are not controlling or at least influencing the conditions of play in the competitive arena you have proactively chosen, your strategy is not working! Change it quickly rather than suffer a long, painful death.

IBM definitely controls the terms of play in the computer arena. Does Unisys? Does Honeywell? Does NEC? Does Fitjusi? Does Wang? Digital and Apple are trying to influence the terms of play. Will they succeed? Time will tell.

AT&T used to control the telecommunications sandbox. Does it today?

Does MCI? Probably not? Does U.S. Sprint? Definitely not. Does any-body? Probably not. Who will eventually? Time will tell. In the meantime several players will make attempts and several will come and go before a new sandbox with clearly defined terms of play emerges.

The gurus that espouse competitive strategy as the tool to manage an organization successfully are, in our opinion, taking a very myopic view of business and the reasons that businesses succeed or fail. These gurus usually ascribe to the "value chain" concept. This concept suggests that you compare your "system" of bringing your product to its intended user to that of your competitors. The suggestion is then made that if you wish to remain competitive, you should be looking for ways to "add value" into as many steps of the chain (thus "value chain") as possible. There obviously is some rationale to this concept. However, by adding value to each com-ponent of your chain may never give you a competitive advantage or may give you a temporary advantage that could quickly disappear. This might happen because you may be trying to add value randomly to the wrong parts of your business or to areas that competitors can quickly duplicate. In other words, you might not be adding value or competitive advantage to areas that are of strategic importance to you. As a result, you will always be in a reactive mode and not be in control of the "sandbox."

The way to control or influence the sandbox is not to deal with a com-petitor by trying to come up with better competitive tactics on a product-by-product or market-by-market basis, but by managing the overall *busi-ness strategy* of that competitor. Another important observation we made while working with CEOs running successful organizations was that many didn't think that having competitors or not having competitors would greatly alter the success or failure of their strategy. They seem to think that *their* own actions, and not those of a competitor, are the cause of their success for failure.

In our judgement, the "competitive" gurus fail to recognize two impor-tant elements of strategy.

1. That competitive activity is only *one* element of strategic analysis and not the exclusive one.
2. That there is a major difference between *business strategy* and *competitive tactics*.

Our suggestion is that the development of a strategy for the business requires a different process than that of competitive analysis and should be done *before* any attempt to develop competitive tactics. Your compet-itors may not be the ones you think!

In the following chapters we will share with you a strategic process that we saw successful strategists utilize to develop their strategy together with a strategic vision for their organization. We will also introduce you to several such CEOs and show how they have used this process to manage their companies. Some of these will be in emerging and fast-growing companies who are in areas where they compete with some of the largest multinationals around, yet they are doing very well against these giants because they "control the sandbox" with a clearly-defined, proactive business strategy.

Our suggestion, as you will read further in this book, is that one element of your business is *strategically* more important to your company's success and survival than all others. And it is important that every strategist/CEO clearly understand which component that is. It is by knowing what your strategic weapon is that one is able to control or influence the rules of play in the competitive sandbox.

Competitive analysis is *an* element of strategy but not the only one. Sound strategic thinking accompanied by a structured *process* can broaden management's peripheral vision and help them develop a *proactive* and, eventually, more successful strategy. The *process* we saw successful CEOs use is called *strategic thinking* and is described in the remainder of this book.

FOUR

What Is Strategic Thinking?

Much has been written in the last few years about the subject of *strategy* in corporations. A proliferation of literature and books have been published with titles such as Strategic Planning, Strategic Management, Management Strategy, Strategic Marketing, and the like.

As we perused through all that literature, we noted two important distinctions.

First, every author that used the word "strategy" used it in a different context. Some view strategy as the objective and "tactics" as the means. Others viewed the goal as the objective and "strategy" as the means or tactics. Still others differentiated between strategy and tactics on the basis of time—strategy being long-term thinking and tactics being short-term or operational. The word "strategy" seems to have become the most abused word in the business vocabulary.

Second, most authors writing on the subject were *outsiders* looking into organizations *after the fact*. They were people who had come to their conclusions by examining the actions of a company post-mortemly and with very little or no contact with the executives of those firms.

With this in mind we decided to proceed differently. We decided to go and talk to people who *run* organizations—chief executives—in an attempt to determine what strategy means to them and *how* they do it. We interviewed dozens of CEOs in all sizes and types of businesses and eventually we even sat in on their strategy sessions with their management teams. As a result, the concepts and process described in this book are a reflection of the *thought process* we saw these people using, if not consciously, at least intuitively and sometimes in an unstructured manner. Peter Drucker, the guru of management science, stated in one of his books, "Every practice rests on a theory, even if the practitioners themselves are unaware of it."

Our approach to this subject, which we have chosen to call *strategic thinking*, has been to identify the *key factors* that dictate the *strategy* and *direction* of an organization together with the *process* that the CEO, the strategist of that organization, uses to set direction. Our focus has been to concentrate on what is meant by *direction* together with the *methodology* used by the CEO and the management team to determine that direction.

Let us initially explore the subject of *direction*. What does it mean to set direction? Or chart the future course? Or set the strategy? To answer this, we must study what goes on inside the heads of people who run organizations. Each person that leads an organization, large or small, has a *concept* or *vision* of what that organization should look like sometime in the future. And it is the pursuit of this vision that engages the efforts of that leader and his colleagues and employs and deploys the resources of that organization. Every company is founded and perpetuates itself on a *key concept* or business idea.

Alfred Sloan, ex-CEO of General Motors and one of the best corporate strategists of this century, said in his book *My Years with General Motors*,

Every enterprise needs a concept of its industry. There is a logical way of doing business in accordance with the facts and circumstances of an industry, if you can figure it out. If there are different concepts among the enterprises involved, these concepts are likely to express competitive forces in their most vigorous and most decisive form.

In an article entitled "How Entrepreneurs Maintain Their Imprint," *Venture* magazine alluded to this concept when it said, "When a company grows too large to respond to its founder's personal touch, it is still shaped by the entrepreneur's vision."

The emergence of NEC, one of Japan's foremost companies, as a world power is attributed to the vision of Koji Kobayashi, its chief executive for over twenty years. That vision, stated twenty-four years ago, was the convergence of "computers and communications." As a result of this "vision," NEC has positioned itself in the forefront of the revolution that is now happening. AT&T, on the other hand, was caught by surprise and outside forces drove it into divestiture. In another article in *Scandinavian Business World*, it was said about P. Andreassen of ISS (Denmark), "He combines *vision* with down-to-earth sense."

Ralph Scurfield, chief executive of Nu-West Group, a real estate and petroleum conglomerate in the U.S., Canada, Europe, Asia, and Australia described his role in a recent interview:

I like to think that my role as the President is to paint maybe half-a-dozen pictures of what the company might look like five years and maybe 10 years from now; hang these on the wall in front of our directors and other advisors and say, here is what we think we should look like, are there any of these pictures you like?, they tend to say I like that, but there's something here that I don't quite like and we end up with a composite. Out of that composite, we try to create something that isn't really mine; it's a product of all our board and senior management.

In a *Harvard Business Review* article on forward planning, Henry Mintzberg made the following observations:

Strategy is the organization's "conception" of how to deal with its environment for a while. If the organization wishes to have a creative, integrated strategy . . . it will rely on one individual to conceptualize its strategy, to synthesize a "vision" of how the organization will respond to its environment. A strategy can be made explicit only when the vision is fully worked out, if it ever is. Often, of course, it is never felt to be fully worked out, hence the strategy is never made explicit and remains the private vision of the Chief Executive.

Since Mintzberg's article, our own work has shown that a *vision* can be made explicit if the chief executive and his management have a *process* to formulate that vision. This vision then becomes, in our terms, a *strategic profile* for the company. Such a profile becomes the target which guides the behaviour of that organization and thus, its *strategy* and *direction* for a certain period of time. The *strategic profile* is then used by top management as a test-bed for their daily and ongoing decisions.

Decisions that "fit" inside the parameters of this profile are taken and implemented while decisions that do not "fit" the profile are rejected. *Strategic thinking*, then, is the *type of thinking that goes on within the*

mind of the CEO, the strategist, to shape and clarify the organization's future strategic profile. Strategic thinking is different from either *strategic planning* or *operational planning,*. In fact, strategic thinking is the *framework* for both the strategic and operational plans.

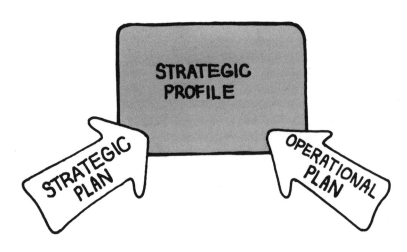

To explore this concept further, strategic thinking can be described as the type of thinking that attempts to determine *what* the organization should look like. In other words—the *strategy*. Operational planning, and even what has become known as strategic planning, is the type of thinking that helps us choose *how* to get there. To illustrate the difference between the two types of thinking, we can develop the following matrix with the *what* on the horizontal axis and the *how* on the vertical axis. We can complete the matrix by further dividing each axis into *good* (+) strategic thinking and *poor* (−) strategic thinking as well as good (+) operation or strategic planning and poor (−) operational or strategic planning.

STRATEGY (What)

	+	−
+	A	B
−	C	D

OPERATIONS (How)

Even as outsiders, we can look at organizations and companies and find four types that exist which practice these two skills with various degrees of effectiveness.

In the "A" quadrant, we find companies which do both very well. They have developed a *clear profile* or strategy and they manage their business on an ongoing basis very well.

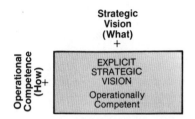

Companies that fall into this quadrant are IBM, Sony, Daimler-Benz, Harrod's, Johnson & Johnson, Honda, Boeing, and Proctor & Gamble.

In quadrant "B" we find companies which have been successful by managing their ongoing operations effectively but which do not always know *where* they're going.

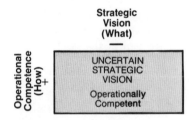

Generally speaking, many of the companies in the United States have been in this quadrant since the early 70s.

In the "C" quadrant, we find the opposite situation. Here there is a very clear strategy but management has difficulty implementing it operationally.

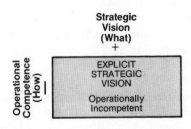

The personal computer producers are a good example of companies who know their strategy very well but the dynamics of that industry are such that the winners and losers vary greatly from year to year. The fortunes of these companies have swung up and down like yo-yos. Witness the experience of corporations such as Osborne, Vector, and Commodore.

The last quadrant is the worst of both worlds. Here we find organizations who do both poorly.

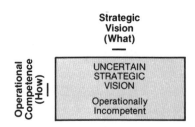

Companies that fall in this quadrant usually don't survive very long and thus it is difficult to generate a long list. But two companies currently attempting to come out of this quadrant are Chrysler and ITT. For many years, Chrysler has not known whether it should compete with Ford or General Motors at one end of the spectrum or with Toyota or Datsun at the other end. Although Chrysler has attempted to drastically improve its operational effectiveness in the last few years, we doubt that its strategy and eventual profile is any clearer than before.

Which quadrant is your organization in?

Although we would all like to say that we are in the "A" ($^+_+$) quadrant, most of our clients readily agree that they fall in the "B" ($^-_+$) one—that is—they are effective operationally but don't always know what direction they are pursuing. As a matter of fact, our experience shows that almost 70%–80% of companies are in that position.

Surprised? Not really when we explore some of the reasons. And there are three major ones.

First, most people who lead and manage organizations got there through the operational ranks. They were promoted from one level to the next because of their operational skills. They were good managers and made good operational decisions. They did not spend much time thinking about, or charting, the direction of the company. As a result they have not acquired the skill of setting direction and being the organization's strategist. That skill takes time to develop.

A second factor that shakes management out of its operational thinking boots is when a company starts going into markets that represent unfamiliar terrain. This occurs when the domestic market peaks and they explore expansion into other geographic markets and countries where the rules of the game are different. Again, the need for management to think strategically surfaces.

Working both sides of the Atlantic we have come to respect the strategic thinking ability of Europeans—particularly the Germans and Swedes. These two countries export the majority of their GNPs and they have a long track record of doing business outside their natural borders. This has forced them to think much more carefully about products, markets, and the allocation of resources. Sweden, with a population of only fourteen million, has twenty companies among *Fortune*'s 500.

Third, there is a tendency when a large domestic market is at our disposal to pursue only two elements from an operational point of view—*market growth* and *market share*. As long as the market grows and we can find new ways to increase our share, we will do well—and thus there is little reason to think about strategy and direction. Momentum alone will carry us forward. This has been the case in the United States during the 60s and 70s. Only in the last few years has the economy become more complex and the need to allocate resources more carefully has given rise to the need to think more strategically.

The strategic thinking *process*, therefore, can be described as the type of thinking that attempts to determine *what* an organization should look like. Strategic planning systems simply help choose *how* to get there.

Strategic thinking is the link to the development of a strategy and a description of the organization's future profile in terms of products, users, and markets as a result of that strategy. Management must have a clear notion of *what* they want their organization to look like in the future before they can determine *how* to get there. Once this is achieved, then the commitment of others can be obtained to that *one* direction.

Strategic thinking is a fresh approach to the subject of strategy. It identifies the key factors that dictate the direction of an organization together with the process that the management of that organization uses to set direction. Strategic thinking involves an organization's key executives directly in the process in order to obtain their commitment and the involvement of others who will be called upon to implement the strategy on a daily basis.

It's a process that extracts out of the minds of people who run the business their best thinking about what is happening in the business, what is happening in the environment, and how to position the business in view of those highly *qualitative* variables (opinions, judgments, and even feelings)—not the *quantitative* ones.

The strategic thinking process is a framework, which helps management produce a profile of *what* the organization wants to become, which then helps them make vital choices, such as which products to pursue and not to pursue, which markets to seek and not to seek, and which customers to offer and not offer our products to. It enables management to position the corporation in order to survive and prosper within a constantly changing environment.

Only when management has consciously discussed and debated the following questions can they start to make operational and strategic decisions to pursue that *profile*:

- What is giving the organization its momentum?
- What has led it to its current scope of products?
- What has led it to its current scope of geographic markets?
- What has led it to its current scope of users or customers?
- What should propel it in the future?
- What business concept are we pursuing?
- What *current* products should receive more emphasis in the future? Less emphasis?
- What *current* geographic markets should receive more emphasis in the future? Less emphasis?
- What *current* users or customers should receive more emphasis in the future? Less emphasis?
- What *new* products should receive more emphasis in the future? Less emphasis?
- What *new* geographic markets should receive more emphasis in the future? Less emphasis?
- What *new* customer or user groups should receive more emphasis? Less emphasis?
- What parts of the business should receive more resources? Fewer resources?
- Does the present organizational structure support this new direction? If not, how should it be changed?
- What are the *critical issues* that must be managed to make the *future profile* a reality?

Strategic thinking is the difference between *planned* growth and growth by momentum only. It is a synopsis of the *conscious* and *systematic* analysis of certain variables that shape management's conclusions about the future. Identifying these variables and building a forum within which these can be discussed objectively is not an easy task. Many obstacles present themselves. It was a study of these obstacles, and sometimes misconceptions about forward planning, that intrigued us next.

FIVE

The Obstacles and the Misconceptions

If the objective of any company is to be in quadrant "A" (clear profile and operationally effective), then the next question has to be: why are they not there? This question led us to probe into the obstacles that get in the way of good *strategic thinking*. Let's explore what these are.

THE STRATEGY SUFFERS FROM "FUZZY VISION"

The first observation we made about the behaviour of people in top management positions is that they spend a lot of time together—in various meetings and on various committees. Some estimates run as high as 80–85% of their time is spent meeting—together. In the course of those meetings, managers talk to one another. One would expect, after all that talking, that the direction of the company would be clear, that they would all share the same vision, particularly after so many years of having worked together. Yet, in spite of this, an interesting phenomenon occurs when each member of the management team is asked to describe the company's future profile and direction. Each person has a different perception!

Each person's vision is slightly different than his colleague's, in spite of the amount of time they spend *together*. These different perceptions of the

company's future are due to the fact that everyone, to some extent, suffers from tunnel vision. Each person sees the company's future profile from one's own perspective and function. One member of a management team that we recently worked with expressed it accurately when he said, "The reason I see the company's future profile as a triangle is because I've been up to my neck in nothing but triangles for 15 years."

OPERATIONAL THINKING DOMINATES MANAGEMENT'S TIME

Even when there is an "unspoken" strategy in existence in a company, there are many interpretations of it. Delving into this phenomenon a little further, we find that the reason is simple—most of the time management spends in meetings is spent discussing operational issues and *not* strategic ones. They always address the "how" of running the business, not the "what."

Operational

Strategic

There are usually a lot of fires that need putting out and those are urgent issues that attract everyone's attention.

REACTIVE VERSUS PROACTIVE STRATEGY

As a result there is a tendency to slip into a *reactive* management mode rather than a *proactive* one. The corporate profile starts being shaped by outside forces rather than by management. These forces can be governments, competitors, unions, and even customers. The environment or competitors, not management, molds the company's direction and strategy.

We once worked with a large utility company that perceived their business and their strategy to be completely shaped by the rules and regulations of the government. They were convinced of this because they were spending some 60% of their time in front of various government agencies and committees, trying to answer questions coming from a variety of different pressure groups. The other 40% of their time was spent reacting to these pressures.

The U.S. automobile industry has been in the same state for the last fifteen years. During this time, their strategy has been set and managed by the Japanese. Many outside forces will gladly take over the direction of your company should you abdicate your right to do so yourself.

NO CRISIS . . . NO STRATEGY!

Another obstacle that impedes strategic thinking is that when times are good . . . who needs to think about where they are going?

The need to think about direction usually surfaces *after* a crisis. General Electric, which is highly regarded for its strategic planning process, did not become concerned about this kind of thinking until the disaster they had

in the computer business in the early 70s when they wrote off several hundred million dollars.

Worldwide, the whole subject of strategy has taken on much more importance in the last few years because of the oil crisis of 1974 and the accompanying uncertainty for the economies of most countries and their industries.

SHORT-TERM VERSUS LONG-TERM?

A fifth obstacle is that many executives associate strategic thinking as *long-term* thinking and operational planning as short-term. Our work indicates that neither type of thinking is time-related.

There are some strategic decisions that can be made which will have a short-term impact and there are operational decisions that can have long-term effects.

The nature of the industry determines the timeframe of both the strategic and the operational thinking. In the oil industry, one must look ahead forty to fifty years because the development of energy resources is a long process.

In the garment industry, on the other hand, one may not want to look further ahead than the next fashion cycle—six months or less!

A bias that our firm has developed against operational planning systems being used in many organizations is the adoption of the five-year business plan. Somehow the business community has developed a fixation around a five-year planning cycle. What is so special about five years? Shouldn't our planning be more related to our strategic timeframe? All that is done with the five-year plan anyway is to update the first year and guess at the last four years. Strategy development and review is not amenable to an annual cycle since the environment is not that predictable. Tying strategy formulation to annual budget exercises ensures failure.

BOTTOM UP OR TOP DOWN PLANNING?

Most "strategic" or operational planning systems are bottom up. Every department head is asked to make his recommendation of revenues and expenses for the next year. These systems start in the bowels of the organization and work their way up.

The strategy of a company, in our opinion, must come from the top and go down. The only people who have a right to articulate the direction of the corporation are the people who have a real stake in that organization, and have to live with the results of their choices and the direction in which they take their company. By using a bottom-up approach, top management abdicates its prerogative to develop an integrated corporate strategy.

ROSE-COLORED GLASSES

Another difficulty between long-range operational planning systems and the strategic thinking process is that because the planning systems are bottom-up exercises, most of the numbers that come to senior management are highly optimistic. When management is finally faced with all numbers, the world looks very rosy and the only thing top management does is shave the numbers a bit.

In fact, what happens is that at every level of management, another degree of optimism is added on. Everybody has to make it better, each adding "x" percent to the forecast. Planning systems can't help set direction. Since they start from the bottom, top management are the last people to get involved in the process. when the numbers hit them, that's it. All they can do is react.

A LAST OBSTACLE IS THE PROCESS ITSELF

Although most companies have very sophisticated operational planning processes and systems, they do not have a *formal process* of strategic thinking.

As a result, even when they do wish to spend some time at the "mountaintop retreat" to think through "where they are going as a company" they usually do not have a process or methodology and early into their discussions they are back discussing operational issues. Some companies have attempted to develop a process but they usually combine strategic and operational issues together and thus make the exercise laborious and confusing. Our suggestion is that the processes are *different* and therefore should be *separated*. The factors and elements studied and evaluated in the strategic thinking process are not the same as in the operational planning process. For this reason, different time should be allotted to each process. Again Milton Lauenstein concurs.

Management should understand that strategic planning encompasses two distinct functions: long-range planning and strategy formulation. Confusing these two activities has contributed to the sorry record of strategic planning. They are better performed separately.

A comparison of each process might help to bring the differences into sharper focus.

Comparison of the Long-Range
Operational System to the Strategic Process

Operational or Long-Range Planning	Strategic Thinking
• *Extrapolation* This process extrapolates forward the organization by adding etimates of growth. It does nothing to change the nature or direction of the company.	• *Framework* This process establishes a framework or profile against which ongoing decisions are tested. It reviews and questions the current direction and sets the future direction which may be different than today's.
• *Bottom Up* This process usually starts in the lowest departments of the organization and works its way up.	• *Top Down* Only one group of people has the right and the obligation to shape the company's future direction and that is top management.
• *Usually Optimistic* A bottom-up process produces numbers and assumptions that are usually optimistic. Managers faced with such presentations find it difficult to assess or evalute the meaning of these plans and end up "shaving" or "trimming" the numbers rather having any meaningful input.	• *Realistic* A framework or profile developed with the full participation of management and their knowledge and expertise becomes a better test-bed for the allocation of resources.
• *Sometimes Erroneous* No one in his right mind will project himself out of existence! This is human nature. Let us assume you have 4 divisions. Two are doing well and two are not. You have set a goal of 8% real growth. Here is what a bottom-up process will produce: The two divisions that are doing well will come in at 7.7% and 7.9% respectively. They will shave their estimates knowing that you will be back for more. The two that are doing badly will come in at 8.1% and 8.3%, justifying their existence. And guess what year of the five-year plan that will be achieved in? Right! The fifth year. This is known as "hockey-stick" planning.	• *Guidelines for Emphasis* A good Strategic Thinking process will produce a profile for the company which can then be used to determine which areas of the business will receive more and which areas will receive less emphasis. The process, therefore, needs to be interactive between levels of management, so that managers whose areas will receive fewer resources in the future are still committed to the direction chosen by management.

• *Nothing Is Eliminated*
Many of our clients who rely heavily on a bottom-up process tell us quite candidly that they have difficulty "pruning" or eliminating product lines or services. This is due to the pressure towards "justification" that this process encourages.

• *Internal Data*
This process uses primarily internally generated data, most of it historical in nature. As a result, the process is objective and based on projections. It requires long and exhaustive studies with a heavy numerical base. It is a *quantitative* evaluation of the business and highly *introspective*.

• *Better Balance*
This process produces a clear list of products and markets that need to be trimmed together with a clear rationale as to why this needs to be done.

• *Internal Plus External Data*
This process incorporates an assessment of both the internal and external environment. It is highly subjective since it is the personal perceptions of each member of the management team. Most of the data required is simple and easy to retrieve since it is stored in each person's head. The key is to tap that knowledge and bring these perceptions into an objective forum. This process is *qualitative* evaluation of the business and its environment and thus both *introspective* and *extrospective*.

A clear *strategic profile* enables an organization to *focus* its resources for optimum performance. That focus is achieved by the systematic analysis of the internal and external environment in which the organization lives. Management does not always have a *conscious process* for determining *what* they want their organization to look like.

This is where we focused our attention. We have concentrated on exploring and documenting the *process* required to assist management chart the future direction of their organizations. We have developed this process with the objective that it should be simple, practical, and visible . . . and the heart of the process is the identification of what gives a company's strategy its momentum . . . the *driving force*.

SIX

The Heart of Strategic Thinking: The Driving Force

What is the reflection, in physical terms, of an organization's strategic profile?

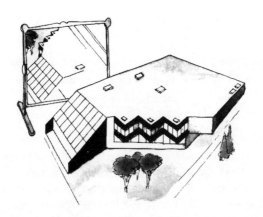

Such is the question to ask if one is interested in knowing what a company's strategy is. The reflection of *what* an organization is or wants to be can be seen in several physical elements. These include:

• People	• Suppliers
• Buildings	• Earnings
• Plants/Factories	• Users
• Products/Services	• Dealers
• Markets	• Shareholders
• Customers	• Balance Sheets
• Assets	• Advertising/Promotion

Of this list, however, the key components of the company's profile are *products*, *markets*, and *users*. The other items are either inputs to, or outputs from, the desire to offer certain products to certain users in certain markets.

Kodak, for example, recently announced that in the next ten years, it is going to hire ten electronic engineers to every one chemical engineer, which is completely opposite to what it did since its origin as a company. What does that say about Kodak's future products? Probably that they will be electronically oriented. Such a declaration gives us an indication of the direction in which Kodak will be going.

At this point, the CEO and the management must ask themselves these three important strategic questions if they intend to shape the future "look" of the organization:

- What determines which products are offered and *which are not?*
- What determines which markets are sought and *which are not?*
- What determines which users are sought and *which are not?*

A company's profile is seen in each of the four areas above. Knowing what will *not* get emphasis, and thus resources, is more important than knowing what will. In order to keep the organization "on course," management must know exactly where the line of demarcation is between the activities that its strategy is meant to support and those that the strategy

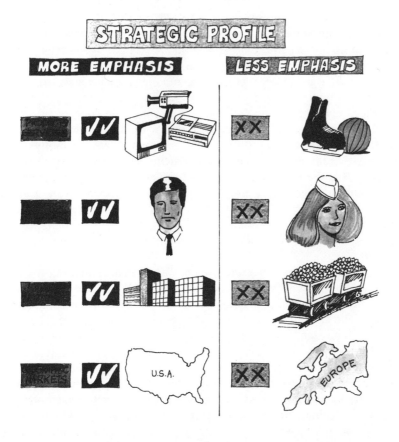

is not designed for. What is it, then, that enables the strategist and the top executives to determine where that line is? The answer to this vital question is the most important element of thinking strategically—it is the concept of *driving force*.

In order to explain, one must look at an organization as a body in motion. Every organization has momentum or motion. Every organization is going forward in *some* direction. Our suggestion is that there is something pushing, propelling, or *driving* it in that direction. The concept of *driving force* or *strategic drive* is that one element or component of a business that drives the organization toward certain products, markets, and customers and thus determines that organization's "look" or profile. The concept of *driving force* is synonymous with a similar idea from Shepherd's Laws of Economics, "Behind each corporation must be a singular force, or motive, that sets it apart from any other corporate structure and gives it its particular identity." It is the identification of what *drives* and gives an organization its momentum in a certain direction that is the key element of strategic thinking. It becomes imperative, therefore, for the top executives of a company to have a clear understanding of the concept of *driving force* if they wish to better manage or even change the direction of their organization.

One test of a company's strategy comes when management is assessing future opportunities. While working with the CEOs of many corporations, we observed that new opportunities were always put through a hierarchy of filters. The final filter always seemed to be the search for a "fit" between the opportunity and one key component of the business. Some CEOs looked for a fit between the products the opportunity brought and the organization's current products—Fiat's acquisition of Alpha Romeo, for example. Others looked for a fit in the customer base or the markets served. Still others looked for a fit of technology or even of selling methods. If a close fit was found, then the opportunity was considered. On the other hand, if the relationship was not seen as a close enough fit, then the opportunity was abandoned. The search for an area of strategic fit, however, varied from one company to another. But it was always the same one in each company. In other words, *one* element of the organization was *driving* its business strategy. The more successful the company, the more the CEO recognized that the organization's strategy was anchored around a key part of its business. It is this *strategic area* that is the heart of a company's business concept and gives it an edge in the marketplace.

Every organization, we found, contains ten important strategic areas:

- Product/Service Concept
- User/Customer Class
- Market Type/Category
- Production Capacity/Capability
- Technology
- Sales/Marketing Method
- Distribution Method

- Natural Resources
- Size/Growth
- Return/Profit

Although all ten of these components are present in most organizations, only one of these is *strategically* most important to a company, and is the engine that propels, or *drives*, the company forward to success. Unfortunately, in many companies, the *key area* that gives a company its *strategic edge* is not always understood by management itself. Once a company's management understands which *driving force* is at the root of the company's strategy, decisions about the types of products, markets, and users that will bring competitive advantage are made more successfully.

Depending on which of these ten strategic areas is most important to a given organization, the decisions it makes about future products, users, and markets will vary greatly. Because each of these ten strategies can lead the organization in a different direction and greatly alter its future profile, management must choose which *one* it will pursue in order to gain competitive advantage. To illustrate the effect of each strategy, we offer the following definitions.

THE CONCEPT OF DRIVING FORCE AND/OR STRATEGIC DRIVE

Product/Service–Driven Strategy

A product-driven company is one that has "tied" its business to a certain "product concept." As a result, this company's future products will greatly resemble its current and past products. Future products will be modifications, adaptations, or extensions of current products. Future products will be derivatives of existing products.

The automobile industry is a good example. The "look" and "function" of cars has not changed for one hundred years and probably will not change for the next one hundred. Thus, Daimler-Benz's and Volvo's business concepts represent product-driven strategies. Boeing also follows this type of strategy. Its business is built around the concept of an airplane and the next product from that company will probably be another flying machine.

User/Customer Class–Driven Strategy

The company pursuing this strategy has decided to "anchor" its business to a *class* of *users*. It then communicates continuously with that user or customer to identify a variety of needs. Products are then made to satisfy those needs. A user-driven company places its destiny in the hands of that customer or user.

Playboy, for instance, is a good example of the *user-driven* concept. This is shown clearly on the cover of its magazine, in the phrase "Entertainment for *Men*." Johnson & Johnson, whose strategy of making products for "doctors, nurses, patients, and mothers" is another example of a company pursuing a strategy anchored to four specific types of users. It follows that J & J will not make products for mechanics, electricians, brick layers, and so forth.

Market Type—Driven Strategy

This company is one that has "anchored" its business to a describable or circumscribable market type or category as opposed to a class of users.

An example of the *market-driven* concept is offered by American Hospital Supply, which caters to the needs of *hospitals* and thus offers a wide range of products that all end up inside of a hospital, the market it has tied itself to.

Production Capacity/Capability—Driven Strategy

This company usually has a substantial investment in its production facility and the strategy is to "keep it running" or "keep it full." Therefore, such a company will pursue any product, customer, or market that can optimize whatever the production facility can handle. Paper mills, hotels, and airlines are good examples of capacity-driven organizations. Keeping the facility at full capacity is the key to profits. Print shops are another class of business pursuing this strategy. A printer will tend to accept any job that the presses can handle, and optimizing the use of those presses leads to profit.

Technology—Driven Strategy

This organization uses technology to gain competitive advantage. It fosters the ability to develop or acquire hard technology (e.g., chemistry) or soft technology (know-how), and then looks for applications for that technology. When an application is found, the organization develops products and infuses into these products a portion of its technology, which brings differentiation to the product. While exploiting this edge in a particular market segment, it looks for other applications in other segments. Technology-driven companies often have "solutions looking for problems" and usually create brand new markets for their products. "The funny thing about this business," says CEO Edson de Castro of Data General, "is that things are designed and brought out when no market exists"—a syndrome that a technology-driven company frequently encounters. "It's always been technology that has driven this company," de Castro adds. Sony, DuPont, and Polaroid are other examples of technology-driven companies. Du-

Pont's invention of nylon led it to market segments as diverse as nylon stockings, nylon shoes, nylon thread, nylon sweaters, nylon fishing line, nylon tires, and nylon-laminated packaging materials. The only thread between all these diverse businesses is that they all stem from one technology—nylon.

Sales/Marketing Method–Driven Strategy

This company has a *unique* way of getting an order from its customer. All products or services offered *must* make use of this selling technique. The company does not entertain products that cannot be sold through its sales method, nor will it solicit customers that cannot be reached through this selling or marketing method. Door-to-door direct selling companies such as Avon, Mary Kay, Amway, and Tupperware are good examples.

The direction of these companies and the products and markets they pursue is determined by their selling method. Amway or Tupperware would never operate in an area where door-to-door selling is prohibited. Their decisions regarding future products are also determined by their selling method. Whatever their salespeople can place in their carrying bags will determine the nature of the product these companies promote.

Distribution Method–Driven Strategy

Companies that have a *unique* way of getting their product or service from their place to their customer's place are pursuing a distribution method-driven strategy. Telephone operating companies, with their network of wires from their switches to the outlets in the walls of your home or office, are an example. A telephone company will only entertain products or services that use or optimize its unique distribution system. Food wholesalers are another example. Department stores such as Sears are a third. Sears' jump into real estate and financial services is an attempt to optimize the use of the company's distribution system. Karl Eller, chairman of Circle K convenience stores—the nation's fastest growing chain—has a very clear understanding of his company's driving force: "We're a massive *distribution system*. Whatever we can push through that store, we will."

Natural Resource–Driven Strategy

When access to or pursuit of natural resources is the key to a company's survival, then that company is natural resource-driven. Oil and mining companies are classic examples.

Size/Growth–Driven Strategy

Companies that are interested in growth for growth's sake or for economies of scale are usually pursuing a strategy of size/growth. All decisions are made to increase size or growth. LTV and Gulf & Western in the 60s and 70s were examples of companies following this strategy. Peter Grace's "philosophy of size and diversification, often at the expense of earnings" for W. R. Grace & Company is another example. Currently, Wickes & Company seems to be in this mode. Sanford Sigoloff, its CEO, has had a voracious appetite for acquisitions in his quest "to be a $10 billion company by 1990."

Profit/Return–Driven Strategy

Whenever a company's only criterion for entering a marketplace or offering a product is profit, then that company is return/profit–driven. Conglomerates are usually good examples. They are usually organized along the lines of corporate control body with fully autonomous subsidiaries. There are usually few or no links between these subsidiaries except a certain level of profit. Subsidiaries are bought or sold on this criterion alone. ITT, under Harold Geneen, had such a strategy. His dictum of "an increase in quarterly earnings, regardless what" and the subsequent acquisition of some 275 unrelated businesses, showed strategic disregard for all other criteria.

STRATEGIC QUESTIONS

Some key *strategic* questions for the strategist at this point are:

- What is your *current driving force*?
- What should your *future driving force* be?
- What impact will it have on your products, markets, and customers?

The answers we have received from the management teams of client organizations to these questions have been varied and frequently surprising, even to themselves.

OUR EXPERIENCE

In strategy sessions with the top management of many companies in North America, Asia, and Europe, several interesting observations have been noted when discussing the notion of what is driving their strategy.

Exclusive Driving Force

"There is only one driving force in a company—return/profit." The statement that return/profit is the only driving force behind a company's strategy is frequently made. Although companies must produce a profit to survive, profit is not usually their "raison d'être." One *must* eat to live but surely the purpose of life is not eating! Companies *must* be profitable, but most companies are founded around another *driving force* or business concept than that of return/profit.

In that case, the next statement we hear is, "Every organization must be user-driven." The rationale of this statement is that if your products do not fill certain user needs, they will not succeed. Every organization, regardless of which *driving force* propels it, must make products that satisfy the needs of the marketplace. However, that alone does not make it user-driven. In other words, every corporation must be *user-sensitive*, but not all corporations are *user-driven*.

Depending on which *driving force* it is pursuing, each organization is *user-sensitive*, but in a different manner. Here are some examples:

- Product-driven. This organization is user-sensitive in that its people are looking for new users of its current products or else it is looking to satisfy new needs within its current user group with slightly modified products.

- User-driven. This organization is user-sensitive in that its people are in a continuous dialogue, usually with a well-known or captive user, to try to identify unique new needs that the user has which can be satisfied by totally new or different products.

- Technology-driven. This organization is user-sensitive in that its people are looking for users which have applications for a technology that the organization has or is willing to acquire. Once applications are found, then products are designed and developed.

- Production capability/capacity–driven. This organization is user-sensitive in that its people are looking for users which offer products or services with components that can be substituted, replaced, or supplemented with their own.

- Sale/Marketing Method–Driven. This organization is user-sensitive in that its people are looking for new products/services that can be sold to current users through their current selling method or new users that can be reached through the same selling method.

- Distribution Method–Driven. This organization is user-sensitive in that its people are looking for new products/services that could be sold to current users or new users that can be reached through its current distribution system.

Multiple Driving Forces

"There are many *driving forces* in our company." This is another statement we frequently encounter. In fact, if there are six people in the room when we talk about this concept we get seven or more views as to the *driving force*. This is quite natural since everyone suffers from a certain amount of "tunnel vision." The marketing head says, "The only reason we're in business is because of my division's ability to sell the product."

The production head says, "If we didn't make the product at a good cost, you would have nothing to sell." The finance head says, "If I couldn't raise the necessary capital, both of you would be out of business." Although this is a normal reaction, it can be dangerous. It is these different perceptions about the *driving force* behind the company's strategy that contributes to different perceptions about the company's direction and the eventual look of its *strategic profile*.

Unfortunately, on an ongoing basis, these people are making operational decisions that are taking the company one way, and then in another way. The organization ends up zig-zagging its way forward.

Dominant Driving Force

In all of the work we have done so far, *one driving force dominates* in any organization at a certain point in time. It is the identification of which one that dominates now and in the future that is of crucial importance to management. How we identify the *dominant driving force* will be discussed in a later chapter.

Unfortunately, the original *driving force* and business concept are sometimes forgotten or lost in the shuffle of the need to make money. Second and third generation management may not always be aware of the *driving force* behind the company's original strategy and the direction of the organization is changed inadvertently, sometimes for the worse.

Hierarchy of Driving Forces

In a single-product company, there is only one *driving force*. However, in a multi-product corporation there is frequently a *hierarchy* of *driving forces* and *business concepts*. The parent company can have a certain *driving force/business concept* while each of its divisions can also have their own *driving forces/business concepts* which can be different from the parent's and also different from each other's.

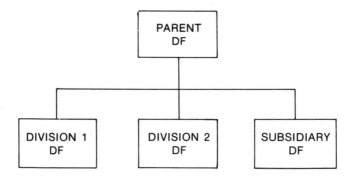

It is important to know what each of these *driving forces/business concepts* are in order to:

1. ensure that the divisional strategies are compatible with the parent's.
2. prevent any overlaps between the division's strategies.

Compatibility between the parent and the division is a *must* because some configurations of *driving forces* cannot exist together. For example, if the corporation is *technology-driven* and one of its divisions assumes a *user/class driving force*, there is bound to be conflict. The corporation is saying that it will only offer products that contain its unique technology while its division is saying that it will respond to the needs of its clients with products that contain anyone's technology. The management of these two units will never see eye-to-eye.

At the divisional level, one must avoid overlaps. Two divisions can sometimes have the same *driving force*. If the business concept articulated around each division's *driving force* is not clear and precise, very frequently this will lead to overlaps in products, markets, and customers.

This situation causes the management of these units to work at cross-purposes. The objective is to have the current blend of *driving forces* in order to breed synergy among divisions and avoid conflicts and overlaps in the marketplace.

The *Driving Force* Limits the Scope of Products and Markets

One reason for knowing clearly which *driving force* dominates is that the *driving force* is the key determinant of the scope of future products, users, and markets. The *driving force* places boundaries on products and markets and violation of these boundaries will abnormally test the organization's skills. Tupperware, the houseware company with the door-to-door saleswomen, is a good example of a sales/marketing method–driven company. To illustrate how one's *driving force* places constraints on one's activities, Tupperware would never open offices in a marketplace where the quality of salesperson required would not be available. Tupperware would also never offer a product for sale that doesn't fit into that salesperson's carrying case.

The driving force can, in some cases, put some physical constraints on certain activities of the organization.

The *Driving Force* Helps Articulate the *Business Concept* of the Organization

As mentioned earlier, every organization originates and perpetuates itself around a key idea or *business concept*. In many organizations, however, that *business concept* is not always clear or well articulated. It usually resides in the mind of the leader and members of that organization get a "feeling" of that concept and the direction of the organization from the nature of the decisions that are accepted or rejected by that leader over a period of time. Most people who head organizations have great difficulty verbalizing their business concept to their colleagues and thus it is reflected by the nature of their actions.

Understanding the concept of *driving force* or *strategic drive* helps managers recognize the conceptual underpinning of that organization's business concept which gives it its momentum and direction.

The business concept of a product-driven organization starts with a clear description of the product. In the automobile industry, we find the following business concepts:

Daimler-Benz:	"The best engineered *car* in the world"
BMW:	"The ultimate driving *machine*"
Volvo:	"Safe and durable *cars*"
Volkswagen:	"People's *car*"

In the computer industry, we find:

| Digital: | "*Computers* for professionals from professionals" |
| Apple: | "A personal *computer* for the home" |

A user- or market-driven organization has a business concept that is focused around the class of user or market it services.

| *Playboy*: | "Entertainment for *men*" |
| Johnson & Johnson: | "Products for *nurses, doctors, patients, and mothers*." |

Sometimes, the *driving force* will be found in the name of the company itself . . . Polaroid . . . obviously a technology-driven company whose business concept was founded on the polaroid technology.

Each of the other categories of *driving force* brings with it a different *business concept* that can more clearly be articulated once the notion of strategic drive is understood.

The *business concept* influences all aspects of a corporation's activities. It determines the scope of products and markets, the organization structure, the technologies required, the type of production facilities, the distribution channels, the marketing and selling techniques, and even the type of people employed. Basically it sets the tone, climate, and behaviour of an organization.

The following chart compares the behaviour of organizations with three distinct *driving forces*.

The Driving Force Dictates Corporate Behaviour

	Product DF	User/Market DF	Technology DF
Organization **Sales**	• By product line • Very strong and aggressive, "push" product • Strong product knowledge	• By user class • Concentrate on distribution (trade)	• By type of technology • Look for application opportunities • Consultative selling
Market Research	• Side-by-side product comparisons	• User interviews • User tells what is needed	• Screen industries • Seek to replace existing technologies
Advertising/ **Promotion**	• Product features/ benefits	• Appeal to user • Build product/ brand loyalty	• Improved benefits • New uses
R & D	• Emphasis on "D" • Customers can't invent—only take modifications to close gaps or reduce complaints • Few disciplines	• Customers invent needs and sometimes the product as well • Multi-disciplinary skills • Outside disciplines often called upon	• Emphasis on "R" • Spend larger % than average on basic or applied research • Specialist skills
Manufacturing	• Go for volume	• Buys or makes product from several sources or in non-related facilities	• May contract out
Areas of **Excellence**	• Product development "D" not "R" • Sales skills (push the product)	• Market research (user knowledge) • Consumer loyalty (Pull the user)	• Research "R" not "D" • Applications marketing

The owner of a Swedish ferry line, who had just discovered that his company was production capacity–driven said, "Now I know why we're forever chasing customers"—the typical behaviour of an organization driven by the need to keep the ships full on every sailing.

Without a clear business concept determining strategic direction, the organization can be led on journeys that can be difficult to understand or explain. Such organizations find themselves practising the Christopher Columbus school of management:

when he set off, he didn't know where he was going: when he got there, he didn't know where he was; when he returned, he didn't know where he had been!

Evolution of the *Driving Force*

In most companies we have worked with, there had been an evolution of the *driving force* over a period of time. A technology-driven company at its beginning may find itself products/services–driven later in life. A products/services–driven company may find itself user/class–driven later. Gillette is a good example. When Gillette started offering its original product, the razor, it was obviously product-driven. As a product-driven company, it sought markets all over the world for that product. At some point in time, however, Gillette asked itself "what other products, closely related to the razor, can we offer our user?" And then came the introduction of shaving cream, deodorant, and cologne. Gillette went from a product-driven company to *user/customer class*–driven company.

There is nothing wrong with that if it is a *conscious* decision at the time. The impact of changing the *driving force* is substantial. Changing *driving force* implies a change of strategy and´impacts all of the activities of an organization including: structure, people, sales method, manufacturing, and distribution. Going from razor blades to shaving cream implies that Gillette needed people who knew about fragrances and lotions rather than how to treat steel. If the decision to change the *driving force* and strategy is not a conscious decision, but rather an accident of evolution, the consequences to a corporation can be fatal. *Business Week* published an article on "How Sir Freddie Shot Himself Down." Their key conclusion: "Sir Freddie Laker's original Skytrain *concept* was simple: a walk-on, walk-off discount flight that charged for food and other frills. Laker began adding frills in mid–1979. In the end, the airline was offering five types of fare, including one for an upscale 'Regency' service that was aimed at the business market. In addition to blurring the public's image of Laker Airways, the new services added to the carrier's cost and destroyed the simplicity of the *original concept. He abandoned his strategy of no-frills flying and competed for high fares.*" Laker attempted to change from a *production capacity*–driven company to a *products/services*–driven one, like the major carriers.

A new business concept or strategy brings with it different *areas of excellence* which we may not yet have developed or which we may not be capable of developing. It also brings new competitors which may have tolerated us in a certain market niche but not in theirs. "The final pricing blow was struck by Pan American World Airways Inc. when it slashed its basic fares on the U.S.–London route by up to 66% to match Laker levels."

Another more recent example of a company that is trying to change its strategy and encountering difficulty is DuPont. Historically DuPont's strategy was technology-driven and succeeded in creating a number of new markets by finding applications for a bevy of its technologies such as cellophane, nylon, Freon, and Teflon. With the acquisition of Conoco, however, DuPont has found itself in a different ball game. Conoco is capital intensive and its products are commodities—the exact opposite of DuPont's—which are high value-added and highly differentiated. Recently, to shore-up Conoco, DuPont has let its technology development—its *area of excellence*—slip to the extent that it is now buying technology rather than creating it. This is a sign of future trouble.

Firestone is another company that attempted to change from product-driven (tires) to use/class needs–driven (automobile drivers and motorists). In the late 60s and early 70s the company started offering for sale in its retail outlets a number of products not related to what they had been selling before—tires. They soon found out that you don't sell charcoal broilers and shovels the same way you sell tires and, in the late 70s, they reverted back to their orginal product-driven strategy. They are now back into the business they know best—tires.

The *Driving Force* Loses or Gains Strength

Another observation is that the *driving force* can gain or lose strength over time. Avon, for example, whose *driving force* is its unique door-to-door selling method, discovered a few years ago that many of the housewives being called upon were now returning to the work force as their children left home. As a result, Avon's *driving force* was losing strength as many of their potential clients were no longer home to receive their saleswomen. To correct this deficiency, Avon started advertising, an activity it never had to do before. This activity did not help as it did nothing to keep housewives at home during the day. Recently, it has started selling on the premises of companies where these housewives now work. Their salespeople run "lunch-hour" cosmetic demonstrations. This approach may work better since it provides access to Avon's traditional user.

Exxon's strategy, since its inception, has been natural resources–driven. In the seventies, however, Exxon saw its *driving force* threatened as Saudi Arabia, Libya, and Venezuela nationalized their oil companies and other countries made similar noises. In response to this threat, Exxon has been searching, for several years now, for a *new driving force*. Thus, their leap into the electronic office equipment industry. This leap to date has been very costly and has yet to justify itself. Depending on the nature of the industry, a change of *driving force* is not necessarily a quick transition and can sometimes take several years to accomplish. In the case of an organization the size of Exxon, that transition could have taken decades. In 1985, however, Exxon reevaluated the threat of nationalization, determined it not to be as great as first expected, and rededicated itself to what it knows best—"exploring for oil and gas." In other words, back to its original resource-driven strategy. It shed its office equipment division and, even more recently, its Reliance Electric division which represented another former strategic mistake.

Does Every Company in the Same Industry Have the Same Driving Force?

The answer is not necessarily so. There is a high probability that competitors in the same industry have different *driving forces* and, as a result, behave differently in the marketplace because each is pursuing a different business concept.

In the film industry, for example, the major competitors are Kodak, Fuji, Polaroid, Agfa, and 3M. By their actions in the marketplace, there is strong evidence that Kodak is product-driven while Fuji is production capacity–driven. Kodak succeeds by continuous improvements to its products. Fuji, on the other hand, competes with "me-too" products offered at lower prices. Polaroid is technology-driven.

In the last few years many organizations have adopted the touted strategic planning model developed at General Electric which emphasizes being number one or two in any business to be successful. What works for GE may not necessarily be the approach for anyone else.

Henry Mintzberg had this view about using other organization's models:

If the organization goes the route of systematic planning, I suggest that it will probably come up with what can be called a "main line" strategy. In effect, it will do what is generally expected of organizations in its situation; where possible, for example, it will copy the established strategies of other organizations. If it is in the automobile business, for instance, it might use the basic General Motors strategy, as Chrysler and Ford have so repeatedly done.

Each organization should formulate its own perception of how to deal with its environment and this concept should revolve around the *driving force* which will steer it through that environment.

Evaporating Business Concept

There is a danger within large organizations of losing sight of the business concept being pursued when there is frequent movement of key managers from one department or division to another. Unless each unit's business concept has been thoughtfully formulated and clearly articulated, it can get lost in the shuffle of management musical chairs or evaporate and be forgotten over time.

Two recent examples are Aminoil and Kentucky Fried Chicken. In each instance new CEOs found that the company, when each took over, had "forgotten" its original business concept and was struggling. G.E. Trimble of Aminoil put it this way:

The industry, including us, was getting into mining and other ventures (silver mining, uranium prospecting, oil shale, and tar sands projects). Our new strategy was to divest and concentrate on our best opportunities—*exploring for, and producing oil and gas.*

Aminoil quickly became profitable again and in 8 years increased its market value from $500 million to over $1.5 billion.

A similar problem occurred at Kentucky Fried Chicken. This company, founded by the famous Colonel Sanders, had been very successful selling "chicken cooked in the Colonel's special recipe." In the 70s, under different management, the company started expanding their menu in other foods and the company's fortunes started to go down. When M. A. Miles took over in 1977, he quickly took the company back to its original business concept and "focused on the one product KFC's upstart competitors could not duplicate—pressure-cooked, fried chicken prepared with the Colonel's secret recipe of herbs and spices."

Fortune magazine recently asked the CEOs of some six hundred companies to rank the top two hundred best-managed corporations in the United States. One interesting distinction about all of the top ten companies was that the CEO has been with the corporation twenty years or more while the bottom ten all have had new CEOs brought in from the outside within the past eighteen months. Some have had several CEOs in the last few years.

Again, our experience has shown that whenever there is a change of chief executive there is a period of groping on the part of his key subordinates until the new CEO establishes his direction. It is important that this "groping" does not become "guessing" what that direction is.

There is much to say for well-motivated, forward-looking, seasoned veterans with in-depth knowledge of the business as the best people to run the organization and perpetuate its business concept. Outsiders often lack appreciation for a business concept that has been cultivated over many years or have little sensitivity for the climate, culture, or corporate beliefs that exist within the organization. Sound *strategic thinking* should precede any change of direction.

To us, the heart of *strategic thinking* is the concept of *driving force*. Managing the *direction* of an organization and its strategy then means managing its *strategic drive*. Management must know which *key area* of the business currently propels the organization's strategy and be able to clearly define and articulate its strategy so that it is understood by those called upon to implement strategic and operational plans. Merck & Company, as one of the world's most profitable companies, is a good example of clear strategic focus. As more and more companies in the 1970s diversified, Merck & Company concentrated its businesses on a narrower strategic target—prescription drugs. It sold off its non-prescription drugs and its specialty chemicals division. This more narrowly defined strategic focus allowed it to make better use of its strengths as well as its resources to become *the* leader in its field in *the 1980s*.

Management must also have in place the proper surveillance mechanisms to quickly detect when the *driving force* loses or gains strength. If it is gaining strength, one wants to exploit it further. If it is weakening, then one must explore the possibility of changing the *driving force* and choosing a more suitable one. This is usually a formidable challenge if not done carefully. A key consideration is not only having recognized the need to change but choosing the most appropriate *driving force* to pursue in the future. A good *strategic thinking* process can ease this choice.

SEVEN

Areas of Excellence: Keeping the Strategy Strong and Healthy

One important observation we have made about some of our most successful clients is that their business concept is well-articulated and clearly understood by all members of the organization and even by most outsiders who come in contact with that organization. In fact, the leader of that organization promotes and perpetuates that business concept with missionary zeal.

The strength of a company's business concept is maintained by the deliberate cultivation of *excellence* in two or three areas that are key to the health of that concept.

An *area of excellence* is a skill, capability, or area of expertise and/or competence that an organization deliberately cultivates to a degree of proficiency beyond anything else it does. By extension, an area of excellence is brought to a higher level of proficiency than any competitor's ability to do the same. Of all the things an organization must do well, it should also cultivate its areas of excellence substantially better than the rest.

The deliberate cultivation of these strategically important capabilities, usually two or three of them, keeps an organization's strategy strong and healthy, and gives it an edge versus its competitors. Losing these two or three skills weakens the strategy and eliminates the organization's competitive edge. Which of the ten strategies is being pursued will greatly change the areas of excellence required to succeed.

PRODUCT-DRIVEN STRATEGY

A product-driven company survives on the *quality* of its product. Witness the automobile wars. Who's winning? The Japanese. Why are Americans buying Japanese cars and even willing to pay premium prices for them during the quota restrictions? The answer is simple: the Japanese make better cars.

One only has to go back to the late fifties when cars from Japan came onto the market. Compared to American cars, they were far inferior. But Japanese car manufacturers understood well that in pursuing a product-driven strategy, one area of excellence required was that of *product development*. They strove to improve the product, to make it better and better, to the extent that it eventually surpassed the quality of American cars.

Of the twenty 1985 cars that got the fewest consumer complaints within ninety days of being purchased, fifteen were Japanese. Four were Toyotas with 109 complaints per hundred cars. The best U.S–made car was sixteenth with 171 complaints per hundred cars. The best known names did not make the top twenty. Pontiac Firebird (415 defects), Chrysler New Yorker (408), Chevrolet Camaro (407), and even the Corvette had 386 defects. Recently, this concept has at least resurfaced at Ford. Ford was the most profitable of the "Big Three" in 1986 and Chairman Donald Petersen attributes their success to Ford's rededication to improving the quality and reliability of Ford cars. A recent study showed Ford's cars to be 75% as reliable as Japanese cars, up from 50% in 1980. This demonstrates that Donald Petersen does understand the concept of an *area of excellence* that must be deliberately cultivated to support a product-driven strategy.

A second area of excellence for a product-driven company is *service*. IBM, which also pursues a product-driven strategy, is well aware of this requirement. Ask any IBM client what they admire most about IBM, and ninety-nine out of one hundred will say its service. IBM deliberately invests more resources in its service function than any other competitor, and thus has a considerable edge in response time and infrequency of product failures.

In a product-driven mode, you maintain your competitive advantage by cultivating excellence in *product development* and *service*.

MARKET/USER–DRIVEN STRATEGY

This organization must also cultivate excellence to maintain its strategy, but in dramatically different areas. A market or user-driven company has placed its destiny in the hands of a type of market or a class of users. Therefore, to survive and prosper, it must know the user of its products better than any competitor. *Market* or *user research* is then a required area of excellence. The company must know everything there is to know about its market or user in order to quickly detect any changes in habits, demographics, attitudes, or tastes. Proctor & Gamble, which is consumer-driven, interviews consumers (particularly housewives), over two million times per year, in an attempt to anticipate trends that can be converted into product opportunities. *Playboy* does the same thing by monitoring changes in its subscribers through its magazine surveys each year.

A second area of excellence for a market/user–driven company is *user loyalty*. Through a variety of means, these companies, over time, build loyalty to the company's products or brands from customers. Then they trade on this loyalty. Johnson & Johnson has, over time, convinced its customers that its products are "safe." And it will not let anything infringe on the loyalty it has developed because of this guarantee. Whenever a Johnson & Johnson product might prove to be a hazard to a person's health, it is immediately removed from the market.

The Tylenol case in Chicago was a good example of how highly Johnson & Johnson values its users' loyalty. As soon as the problem surfaced, and even though there was substantial doubt that anything was wrong with the product, which was proven to be the case, the company removed the product from the shelf everywhere in the world. "Experts" then predicted the death of Tylenol because they reasoned that Johnson & Johnson's recall was an admission of guilt. Not so. Three months later, Johnson & Johnson reintroduced the product, showed how the company had eliminated the possibility of tampering, demonstrated that the product was "safe" again, and traded on their users' loyalty to regain sales. Six months later Tylenol once more had the largest market share.

Another example of how good user or consumer-driven companies are at developing user loyalty is Coca-Cola's recent experience in trying to change its formula. Coca-Cola had built so much brand loyalty that its users did not allow the company to change its formula.

PRODUCTION CAPACITY–DRIVEN STRATEGY

When there is a glut in the market, the first thing a paper company does is lower the price. Therefore, to survive during the period of low prices, one has to have the lowest costs of any competitor. To achieve this, an area of excellence required is *manufacturing* or *plant efficiency*. This is why the paper companies are forever investing their profits in their mills—to make them more and more efficient. An industry that has lost sight of this notion is the steel industry in the United States and Central Europe. By not improving their plants they have lost business to the Italians and Japanese, who have done so. One notable exception in the U.S. is Allegheny Ludlum, which has done very well because it has the lowest costs of any steel mill, including the Japanese or Italian mills. As a result its revenues and profits have consistently improved. Allegheny managers are unique in that they know the cost of each of perhaps thirty thousand coils of steel floating around the company's seven plants, at any given stage of production. "The thing that scares me now is that we know our true costs, but competitors don't," says CEO Richard Simmons. "How can they make logical pricing decisions?" ("Allegheny Ludlum Has Steel Figured Out," *Fortune*)

In another industry, textiles, that has lost a lot of ground to off-shore competitors one exception stands out. Guilford Mills in Greensboro, North Carolina, is competing very successfully and the reason is that its chief executive, Charles Hayes, knows that, as a production capacity–driven organization, his company must excel at optimizing manufacturing efficiency. "We can make fabric as cheaply as anyone in the world," he says. "We take that basic commodity, nylon lingerie fabric, and enhance it. The more we can do to it in the manufacturing process, the more we can sell it for and the higher our margins." In order to do this he spends heavily on new equipment—over $36 million over two years to gain the most automated knitting, dying, and fiber plants in the world.

A second area of excellence for this strategy is what we call *substitute marketing*. Production-driven companies excel at substituting what comes off their machines for other things. The paper people are trying to substitute paper for plastic; the plastic people plastic for aluminum; concrete for steel. The same is true in the transportation industry, where the bus companies are trying to replace trains; the train companies the airlines; and so forth.

TECHNOLOGY–DRIVEN STRATEGY

This company uses technology as its edge. Thus, an area of excellence required to win under this strategy is *research*, either basic or applied. Sony, for example, spends 10% of sales on research, which is 2 or 3% more than any competitor. Its motto, "research is the difference," is proof that the company's management recognizes the need to excel in this area.

By pushing the technology further than any competitor, new products and new markets will emerge. Technology-driven companies usually *create* markets rather than respond to needs, and usually follow their technology wherever it leads them.

Merck & Company is another good example of a company whose CEO and chief strategist, Roy Vagelos, knows precisely what area of excellence must be fueled to deliver new products. Merck, at Vagelos' directive, pours hundreds of millions into research, as a technology-driven company should, and has come up with an ongoing stream of new products (five in 1986 alone) in an industry that introduces a new drug about as often as an aircraft manufacturer introduces a new airplane. It has consistently spent a greater share of its revenues on research than the rest of the industry. In 1986, the amount was $460 million, which was more than 11% of sales. Its research teams *excel* and are on the leading edge of science in bio-chemistry, neurology, immunology, and molecular biology. Few other drug companies can match the breadth and depth of expertise Merck has in these areas.

A second area of excellence then is what we call *applications marketing*. Technology-driven companies seem to have a knack for finding applications for their technology that call for highly differentiated products. 3M's use of its coating technology to develop Post-It note pads is a good example.

SALES MARKETING METHOD—DRIVEN STRATEGY

The prosperity of a sales method-driven company depends on the reach and effectiveness of its selling method. As a result, the first area of excellence companies such as Avon and Mary Kay must cultivate is the ongoing *recruitment* of door-to-door salespeople. Mary Kay has had tremendous success in the last few years because it has been able to draw several hundred thousand women to sell its product. Avon's fortunes have suffered because its sales force has dropped considerably during that same period.

The second area of excellence needed to succeed with this strategy is improving the effectiveness of the selling method. Door-to-door companies are constantly *training* their salespeople in product knowledge, product demonstration, and selling skills. Growth and profits come from improving volume through diversity and improvement of sales methods.

DISTRIBUTION METHOD—DRIVEN STRATEGY

To win the war while pursuing this strategy, you must first of all have the *most effective* distribution method. As a result, you must offer products and services that use or enhance your distribution system. Second, you are always looking for ways to *optimize* the *effectiveness*, either in cost or value, of that system. That is your edge. You should also be on the look-out for any form of distribution that could bypass or make your distribution method obsolete.

AT&T is a good example of a company that was caught napping by MCI when MCI found a more efficient method (microwave) for distributing voice signals. Had AT&T been aware of their own driving force, *they* would have been the ones to introduce microwave technology as an alternative distribution method, not MCI. If this was the case, AT&T would still be one company today.

NATURAL RESOURCE–DRIVEN STRATEGY

Successful resource-driven companies excel at doing just that—*exploring* and finding the type of resources they are engaged in. Exxon considers itself to be best at "exploring for oil and gas," and it does this better than any competitor. It was the recognition of this fact that led Exxon to drop its office equipment division. There's not much oil and gas to be found there; plus, that kind of venture requires excellence in areas Exxon does not possess.

Another example is Occidental Petroleum, run by Armand Hammer, who claims that Oxy's unique area of expertise is "finding oil where others have failed. That's the whole history of our company."

John Bookout, CEO of Shell USA, is a good example of a strategist that understands his company's areas of excellence. Shell's particular expertise is "enhanced oil recovery in offshore waters deeper than 600 feet." In this area, Shell has few rivals as he recently explained to *Forbes* magazine. In 1983, Shell drilled a project called Bullwinkle in the Gulf of Mexico at a depth of 1350 feet. Outsiders thought Bookout had lost his mind, particularly since Shell did not spread the risk by taking other partners on the deal. "You can't believe how easy that decision was," he says. "It took us 30 minutes in the boardroom." The reason? Bookout was banking on Shell's area of excellence in deep water recovery.

Many oil companies have lost track of his notion during the last few years and have strayed into areas where they have no expertise. Tremendous difficulties result. Witness Mobil's experience since it acquired Montgomery Ward. It has been nothing but trouble.

SIZE/GROWTH OR RETURN/PROFIT–DRIVEN STRATEGY

Companies which choose either of these two strategies require excellence in financial management. One such area is *portfolio management*. This means proficiency at moving assets around in order to maximize the size/ growth or return/profit of the entire organization.

A second area of excellence is *information systems*. These companies usually have a corporate "Big Brother" group that constantly monitors the performance of its various divisions and, as soon as a problem is detected, an attempt to correct or expunge it is made. Mr. Geneen had such a group at ITT.

Again, each of the other *driving forces* bring with it a need to cultivate areas of excellence substantially different. The importance of understanding this concept is that no organization has the resources to develop excellence in all eighteen areas! Therefore, it must make some serious choices as to which ones to develop and what level of proficiency it must attain in order for its business concept to remain strong and to maintain its edge against its competitors.

Areas of Excellence

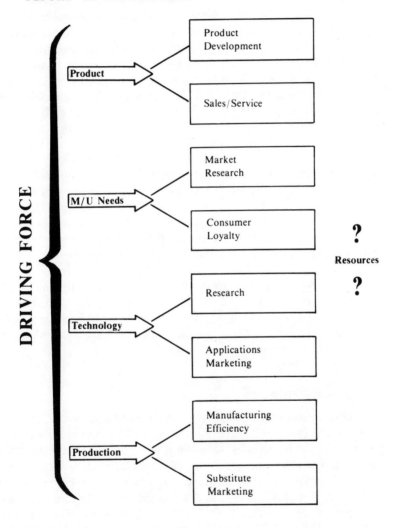

TWO KEY DECISIONS

A company, therefore, has two additional key strategic decisions to make if it wishes to succeed.

First, it must determine which strategic area will drive the business concept and thus the direction of the organization. Then it must decide what *areas of excellence* or *competence* it must cultivate to keep that strategy healthy. These *areas of excellence* should receive preferential treatment, fueling them with more resources in order to develop a level of proficiency greater than any competitor. Once resources are diverted elsewhere, proficiency diminishes and the company loses its edge vis-à-vis its competitors.

Our experience has clearly shown that any strategy can work but that no company can pursue two strategies simultaneously. No organization has the resources to develop excellence in several areas concurrently.

Understanding the concepts of *strategic drive* or *driving force* and *areas of excellence* makes life much easier for the CEO and the management team in terms of the decisions they make about new products, markets, and customers that constitute the future profile of the organization.

Even when a CEO wants to change the strategy of the organization, it is not that simple a task if consideration has not yet been given as to which new areas of excellence will be required to make the new strategy work. Avon is a good example. "We are not a direct selling company. We are a beauty company." That simple statement by CEO Hicks B. Waldron reflects a profound change of direction from a selling method–driven strategy to a product-driven one. The *areas of excellence* required to make Mr. Waldron's new strategy work will be considerably different than the competences Avon has had historically. Let's hope Mr. Waldron has thought this through carefully and that the rest of the organization realizes the implications that will result.

SEDUCED BY OPPORTUNITIES

Too often, organizations get seduced by opportunities that require excellence in areas they don't currently possess and the opportunity is not a success as a result. Sometimes, to make it succeed, the organization will shift its resources in an attempt to develop excellence in new areas. But, in order to do so, it must take resources away from its current areas. This spells disaster. Not only do they not develop the new areas to the required levels of excellence to succeed but they end up losing excellence in their current areas. The net effect is to become a me-too competitor in the new market segment and to make it easier for their competitors in their current business.

Sometimes the opportunity might even turn out to be extremely profitable but still these don't necessarily represent sound strategic fits. R. J.

Reynolds, the cigarette giant, has recently had that experience. A few years ago, in an era when diversification was a corporate craze, Reynolds purchased Aminoil, an oil exploration firm, and Sea-Land Industries, an ocean shipper. Although Aminoil turned out to be extremely profitable for Reynolds, the company has now decided to sell both of these investments. T. J. Wilson, Reynolds' CEO, explained this decision by recently stating to *Business Week* that Reynolds was "consumer-driven" and did not understand these two businesses nor could they transfer the expertise they had to these industries. "A marketing orientation is the common thread running through our business," says Wilson. As a result, Wilson has decided to return to "consumer-driven" businesses where their area of excellence—marketing skills—can be applied even though these businesses may be more competitive. Wilson obviously feels that their marketing excellence is the edge that Reynolds brings to the market. Lesson: diversification is not necessarily good for everyone!

Too often organizations are distracted from what has made them successful. The most successful organizations are the ones where the leader and senior management clearly understand their business concept and fuel the key *areas of excellence* required for success with more resources each year than they give to other areas. They then pursue this business concept with total dedication and without allowing any competitor to attain the same level of excellence in a few key capabilities. As Benjamin Disraeli so clearly noted many decades ago, "The secret to success is constancy of purpose."

Knowing what *strategic area* drives your organization and the *areas of excellence* required to support that strategy is akin to understanding what is the *strategic weapon* that will give you a distinct and sustainable advantage in the marketplace.

Many U.S. multi-nationals are currently losing sight of the notion. The latest fad is to embark on "strategic alliances" with Japanese companies in an attempt to improve their competitiveness. Unfortunately, these U.S. companies are losing sight of their *driving force* and are entering into alliances where they are giving up control of their *strategic weapon*. In the article "Use a Long Spoon" (*Forbes*, 1986), C. K. Prahalad, of the University of Michigan, made a study of eight such alliances and concluded that Western companies had too easily given up control of key technologies to the Japanese. Prahalad suggests that Western companies should think of these deals not as "strategic alliances" but as "competitive collaboration." He explains, "That would alert the organization to what they should protect." He also suggests, "Don't let your partner *underwork your core technology and skills*." If you do so, "Japanese companies will build an ever more complex *competency* base and Western companies will surrender ever more control over their own competitiveness."

We would certainly agree with Prahalad. While working with owner-managed companies, we have noticed that these companies *never* license their *key skills* or *expertise* to anyone. Much more than publicly-run companies, the CEO strategist in these organizations has a very clear understanding as to what area of the business drives the organization's strategy and what *areas of excellence* make that strategy work. And control over this *strategic weapon* is never relinquished!

EIGHT

The Strategic Thinking Process

"Picture-painting," as Ralph Scurfield of Nu-West so aptly described it, is what strategic thinking is all about. Like the master painter, management must know where to start, what paints and brushes to use, and know when the picture is complete. In other words, they must know the *process* of painting. In business terms, management must know and understand the *process* required to develop a strategic profile for the organization. It is this process that we will explore in this chapter.

As mentioned earlier, strategic thinking is a *qualitative* assessment of the business and the environment it faces. As such, much of the data is "soft" as opposed to the "hard" data produced by most planning and analytical tools used in organizations today.

In another *Harvard Business Review* article, Henry Mintzberg gave these additional insights on how chief executives charted the future of their organizations.

Managers' concentration on the verbal media suggests that they desire relational, simultaneous methods of acquiring information, rather than the ordered and sequential ones.

A great deal of the manager's inputs are soft and speculative—impressions and feelings.

What can managers do with this soft, speculative information? They "synthesize" rather than "analyze" it. A great deal of this information helps the manager understand implicitly his organization and its environment, to "see the big picture."

In effect, managers use their information to build mental "models" of their world, which are implicit synthesized apprehensions of how their organizations and environments function. Then, whenever an action is contemplated, the manager can stimulate the outcome using his implicit models.

The environment does not run on planners' five-year schedules; it may be stable for thirteen years, and then suddenly blow all to hell in the fourteenth.

The burden to cope falls on the manager, specifically on this mental processes— intuitional and experiential—that can deal with the irregular inputs from the environment.

The process of strategic thinking described in this chapter has been developed and refined while working with client organizations. It is not a theoretical approach to the subject but rather a tested and tried methodology currently being used by a number of corporations. It places, in logical order, the various elements that management need to consider in order to conduct their strategic thinking in a time-efficient manner. It assembles and collects their impressions and opinions about the environment in order to conceptualize or synthesize a collective vision to deal with that environment.

The first part of this chapter will outline the different components of the process while the second part will deal with the logistics.

THE PROCESS

Our strategic thinking process incorporates eight steps. These are:

1. Clarification of the Current Profile
2. Analysis of Strategic Variables
3. Exploration of Different Driving Forces and Possible Strategic Profiles
4. Development of a Future Strategic Profile
5. Development of Competitive Profiles
6. Testing the Strategic Profile
7. Final Strategic Profile
8. Identification of Critical Issues

STRATEGIC THINKING PROCESS

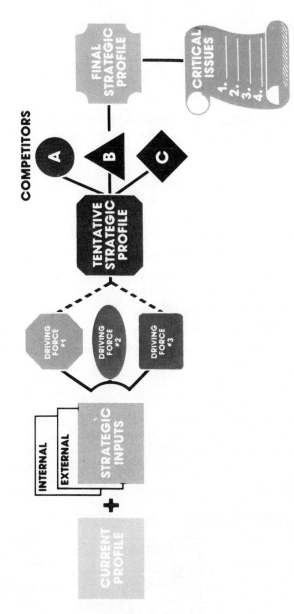

CLARIFICATION OF THE CURRENT PROFILE

The first step in the process is taking stock of where the organization currently is. To do this one needs to take a "photograph" of the organization in its present state.

One needs to know:

- The scope of current products and services.
- How these products or services are grouped.
- The trends or cycles they experience.
- The scope of the geographic areas they serve.
- The user groups they have attracted.
- The growth of these in the last few years.
- Their market share and that of the competition.
- The organization structure in place to support the above product/market division.
- The return of each product/market division.
- The current *driving force*.
- The current *business concept*.
- The current *areas of excellence*.

Collection of the above information provides management with a "snapshot" or *current profile* of the organization. This is the present composition of the organization as it is presently being propelled forward by a certain *driving force*.

ANALYSIS OF STRATEGIC VARIABLES

The old saying "garbage in, garbage out" is very applicable in strategic thinking. The quality of the strategic inputs determines to a great extent the quality of the outcome of such an exercise. However, in order to obtain high quality inputs, there is no need to undertake massive and costly studies about the future and its negative predictions. The best inputs are stored in the minds of the key people who run the company. Future direction is greatly influenced by the experience and perceptions of these people about the internal and external environment in which the organization exists. The trick is to tap this wealth of knowledge and bring it forward in an objective forum.

To do this we have developed a strategic input survey which *each* member of management answers. The survey obtains each person's view on eleven key areas of the internal and external environment.

Internal Environment

Products

- The common characteristics of products or services
- The exceptionally successful products
- The characteristics of their success
- The exceptionally unsuccessful products
- The characteristics of their failure

Geographic Markets

- The common characteristics of geographic markets
- The exceptionally successful geographic markets
- The characteristics of their success
- The exceptionally unsuccessful markets
- The characteristics of their failure

User Segments

- The common characteristics of user groups
- The exceptionally successful user segments
- The characteristics of their success
- The exceptionally unsuccessful user segments
- The characteristics of their failure

Corporate Beliefs

- The principles, beliefs, and values that guide corporate behaviour. More will be said about this item in a following chapter.

Strengths

- The *unique* strengths of the organization
- The strengths possessed to a greater extent than the competition
- Traits that may become strengths later

Weaknesses

- The unique weaknesses of the organization
- The weaknesses possessed to a greater extent than the competition
- Traits that may become weaknesses later

Internal Opportunities

- Short-term internal opportunities
- Medium-term internal opportunities
- Long-term internal opportunities

External Environment

Competition

- Direct competitors (present and future)
- Indirect competitors (present and future)
- Their strengths
- Their weaknesses
- New forms of competition
- Suppliers or customers that may become competitors

External Threats/Opportunities

- Short-term external opportunities/threats
- Medium-term external opportunities/threats
- Long-term external opportunities/threats

Strategic Vulnerability Areas

- Raw materials
- Technology
- Labor
- Legislation
- Capital

From the above categories our strategic input survey consists of forty-two key questions that are asked of each member of the management team. Their answers to these questions are all the data required as a basis for the development of a strategic profile for the organization. The consolidation of the information extracted from each person is the best environmental "scan" one can do. As mentioned before, this information is highly qualitative in nature, but nevertheless, is the foundation of sound strategic thinking.

EXPLORATION OF DIFFERENT DRIVING FORCES AND POSSIBLE STRATEGIC PROFILES

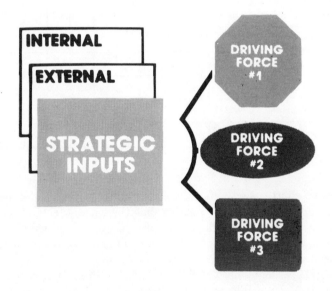

The systematic analysis of the *internal* and *external* environment can provide clues as to whether the existing *driving force* is suitable to that environment. Should there be a need to explore other *driving forces*, the strategic inputs can assist there as well. By establishing a matrix whereby we match the strategic input categories against the nine *driving forces*, management can identify two or three *driving forces* which might be better equipped to handle the various issues raised.

DRIVING FORCES \ STRATEGIC INPUTS	PRODUCTS	MARKETS	CORPORATE BELIEFS	STRENGTHS	WEAKNESSES	INTERNAL OPPORTUNITIES	COMPETITION	EXTERNAL THREATS	EXTERNAL OPPORTUNITIES	VULNERABILITY AREAS
• Products/Services			X							
• User/Market needs	X	X		X		X	X		X	
• Technology		X		X	X			X		X
• Production capacity/capability										
• Sale/marketing method										
• Distribution Method	X		X	X	X		X	X	X	X
• Natural resources										
• Size/Growth										
• Return/Profit						X				

★ Current Driving Force

The above chart suggests that a user/market or a distribution method–driven strategy might be more suitable than the current technology-driven strategy. Having tentatively chosen the two most likely *driving forces* that react well to the strategic inputs, management can now project ahead the type of products and markets each one would lead to. The type of products, markets, and user segments will differ greatly from one strategy to another. Exploring several possible future profiles is a key element of strategy formulation. It allows management to develop a strategy proactively on the basis of comparison to other, less favorable, alternative strategies.

Having drawn these profiles they can now be compared to the current profile and the question arises whether these new profiles are realistic. The most realistic one can then be chosen as a *tentative future strategic profile*.

DEVELOPMENT OF THE FUTURE STRATEGIC PROFILE

The strategic profile of an organization establishes the parameters or boundaries within which it will conduct its business. It is the "vision" in

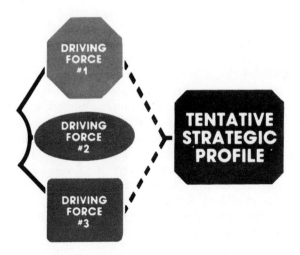

the strategist's mind and what the organization is trying to become.

A strategic profile should be short enough that it can be carried in one's head, and the boundaries should be clear and precise enough that managers can use it daily as a test-bed for their decisions. Like "picture-painters" the master strategist must know what to include in the strategic profile. The following elements are the items that need to be clearly articulated.

Future Strategic Profile

Time Frame

A suitable time period for strategic thinking needs to be agreed upon. As stated earlier there is no rule and it should be determined by the nature of the business.

Driving Force and Business Concept

The category of *driving force* that will propel the organization during this period should be clearly established. This should be accompanied by a short description of the business concept that will be pursued in this mode. Since it is possible for two competitors within the same industry to have the same *driving force* but different *business concepts*, the particular description each one attaches to the *driving force* may influence greatly the direction it pursues. Volkswagen and Daimler-Benz, for example, are both product-driven companies. However, the definition that each gives to its product leads those two automobile companies down different paths in everything they do, including: product design, pricing, advertising, disbution, and manufacturing. BMW and Porsche describe their "product" in yet a slightly different manner which gives each company its own uniqueness and separates them from either Daimler-Benz or Volkswagen.

The description of the *driving force* is the description of the singular *business concept* or purpose of the organization. It is the *conceptual underpinning* of the business which sets the parameters for the scope of products, geographic markets, and user segments.

Although corporations may get very large, the original idea that got them started is usually very simple and can be described in one or two sentences. It needs to be clear and crisp so that it can easily be retained by the dozens, hundreds, or thousands of people who are called upon to perpetuate it. The president of Alcan keeps that company's business concept inscribed on a metal tent card on his desk. It faces the person seated on the other side and it says, simply, "Our product is aluminum." The metal used for the inscription is, of course, aluminum.

Akio Morita's concept of "using technology in ingenious ways" is a good example of a technology-driven business concept which was at the root of Mr. Morita's vision and has been propelling Sony ever since.

A CEO who has difficulty articulating and disseminating his *business concept* will have great difficulty getting his key executives' commitment to any *one* direction. Furthermore, the inability to clearly define and articulate one's business concept leads to the failure to establish an "edge" in the marketplace.

Areas of Excellence

The next elements to clearly establish are those two or three activities within the company that require excellence to a degree greater than any competitor, or to a greater degree than anything else the company does, if the *business concept* is to maintain its strength. Every organization excels in two or three areas and it is this excellence that gives the *business concept* its strength. For a *business concept* to maintain its strength in the future, the *areas of excellence* which fuel this strength need to be identified and cultivated.

A product-driven company, for example, will need to excel at product development in order to improve current products and develop new ones. These skills are normally accompanied by excellent selling skills in order to convince more and more clients to buy its products. The *areas of excellence* vary from one *driving force* to another. Knowing which one we need to perfect will determine how resources are allocated.

Product Scope

Management must now turn its attention to listing the type of current and future products which are suited to this *business concept* and which will receive *more* emphasis in the future. They also list those current and future products which are *not* suited to the *business concept* and will therefore receive *less* emphasis. This short list will serve as a filter for future product opportunities and test these for a "fit." If they fall on the *less emphasis* side, it should serve as a red flag to the company, telling it that it is not organized to support this type of product opportunity and it should not be pursued.

Market/User Scope

The same is done for geographic markets and user groups. In each instance a list is drawn to identify those that *will* be pursued and those that *will not*. Again, the objective is to construct a screen for future market or user opportunities.

Size/Growth Guidelines

The next part of the profile is to clarify the size and growth guidelines for the organization to achieve during the strategic timeframe. The key word here is *guidelines*. These are usually ranges of numbers in such categories as sales, revenues, turnover, and growth.

Return/Profit Guidelines

This category specifies numbers which reflect guidelines for profit and return. The size/growth, return/profit guidelines should be representative of the financial performance required to provide the necessary cash flow to enable the organization to achieve its strategic profile.

Corporate Beliefs

Although *corporate beliefs* are not part and parcel of the strategic profile of an organization, they are an integral part of the strategic thinking of the principals of that organization. The values, beliefs, and principles that these people own go a long way toward setting the tone of corporate behaviour and molding the scope of its products and markets. They are to the strategic profile what the frame is to a painting.

One executive described corporate beliefs as "moral guidelines, written or unwritten, that a company sets for itself in dealing with its environment."

These beliefs exist in every company even though they are not always visible and known. However, once they have been drawn out of top management, our recommendation is always that they accompany any publication of the strategic profile, as they are the moral foundation upon which it is based.

To illustrate their importance, two examples come to mind. We once worked with a tobacco manufacturer who identified as an opportunity, during one of our sessions, the possibility of obtaining distribution in one of the largest department store chains. Since this chain did not carry tobacco products, distribution alone would have meant a sizable initial order and a chance to significantly increase market share. They set about devising an elaborate plan to approach the chain's buyer. By coincidence, we had also worked with the department store and knew that this possibility would never materialize. We informed the tobacco manufacturer of our opinion. "Why?" he asked. The reason was simple. The founder of the department store chain was a devout abstainer and no tobacco or alcoholic products would ever be offered for sale in his stores. His personal belief, then and now, dictates corporate behaviour.

The second example occurred when the author was with Johnson & Johnson in the 60s. Baby oil is one of their products and we started noticing that teenagers and adults used it every spring as a suntanning lotion. It works well when used this way since baby oil has no suncreening ingredient. We saw an opportunity and every spring Johnson & Johnson started promoting its baby oil in the suntan market. They were so successful that within a few years they had the market's largest share. At the same time, however, there was emerging research which indicated that overexposure to the sun might be a possible cause of skin cancer. J & J, at that time and still now, had a corporate belief that said it would "never offer for sale any product that may prove to be a hazard to a person's health." The suntan market experience was violating this belief. A decision was made in 1969 to withdraw all promotional funds and activities from the suntanning market with a resultant loss of 15% in baby oil sales.

These corporate beliefs, known as the Credo, existed then and still dictate corporate behaviour today. *Fortune* magazine once did a story on J & J and a large segment of the article was naturally devoted to "The General's Credo."

The other force that holds J & J together is an improbable one—The Credo, a 291-word code of corporate behavior that has a mystical but nonetheless palpable influence in the company. The Credo is a legacy of "The General," Robert Wood Johnson, the son of one of the founding Johnson brothers and the man who, during his long rule, from 1938 to 1963, shaped the company. Rare is the conversation with a J & J executive in which the Credo does not come up. Several years ago company officers debated for hours before changing a paragraph in the document... Some outsiders might consider the Credo not so much corny, as wrongheaded. It commands that the company service customers first (especially mothers, nurses, doctors, and patients), employees second, the communities in which the company operates third, and the shareholders last of all. J & J has sometimes sacrificed earnings in what is perceived to be the best interest of the customers.

Their behaviour in the recent Tylenol case is another good example of adherence to this Credo.

When one looks at the scope of J & J products and markets, one can look to the Credo as a key filter to the choices this company has made in these areas of its strategic profile.

DEVELOPMENT OF COMPETITIVE PROFILES

COMPETITORS

As outsiders, it is still surprisingly easy to determine the *driving force* of one's key competitors. One only needs to look at their actions in the marketplace. By knowing their *driving force* one can then *anticipate* what they will do in the future. We were working with a film manufacturer not too long ago and they identified that one of their major competitors was production capacity–driven. In a soft market such an organization usually resorts to price cutting in order to maintain volumes. Our client anticipated this type of behaviour from that one competitor and, sure enough, one week later that is exactly what that competitor did. This time, however, our client was ready and their action had little effect.

The next step in this process is the construction of *future profiles* for the three or four major competitors. By identifying each competitor's *driving force*, one can easily anticipate which products, markets, and user groups they will pursue and which ones they won't. These profiles will be valuable to have in order to proceed to the next step—the test step.

TESTING THE STRATEGIC PROFILE

The test of the future strategic profile has three parts:

A. Versus the Current Profile
B. Versus the Strategic Inputs
C. Versus the Competitive Profiles

A. Versus the Current Profile

This test consists of comparing the *future strategic profile* to the current profile. The type of questions asked are:

- How large are the gaps between the two profiles?
- What changes need to be made to go from the current product scope to the new product scope?
- What changes need to be made to go from the current market scope to the new market scope?
- What changes need to be made to go from the current user groups to the new user groups?
- What new resources/skills will be required?
- Is it realistic to achieve this within this timeframe?
- How should the strategy and profile be modified in view of the above?

B. Versus the Strategic Inputs

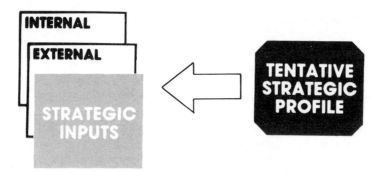

This test consists of comparing the *future strategic profile* to the original strategic inputs about the external and internal environment. The questions asked are:

- Are the organization's unique strengths being exploited?
- Are its unique weaknesses being minimized?
- Are any corporate beliefs being violated?
- Are all major opportunities being exploited?
- Are all major threats being avoided?
- How should the profile be modified?

C. Versus the Competitive Profiles

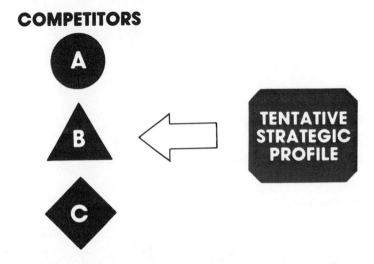

This test consists of comparing the *future strategic profile* to each of the major competitors that will be attracted to your strategy. The questions asked are:

- Is our strategy running up against their strengths?
- Are their weaknesses being exploited?
- How will they react to this strategy?
- How can their actions be counteracted?
- What is driving their strategy?
- How can we offset their areas of excellence?

FINAL STRATEGIC PROFILE

Final Strategic Profile

The three-way test just completed surfaces a number of issues and provides an opportunity to try to "shoot holes" in management's thinking. It also affords them the chance to reshape their strategy and profile one more time before adopting it.

IDENTIFICATION OF CRITICAL ISSUES

Critical Issues

The preceding step will also surface a number of key issues which management will need to resolve if their *future strategic profile* is to become a reality. These *critical issues* are the bridge between the current profile and the final strategic profile. *Setting* the *direction* of the organization has now been achieved. *Managing* that direction now starts and managing that direction on an ongoing basis means the ongoing management of the critical issues.

THE LOGISTICS AND MECHANICS OF THE PROCESS

Before describing *how* we work with this process in a client organization, it is important to say a few words about our role in such an assignment. Our role, as an outside consultant, is *not* to set the direction of the client's organization. We feel quite strongly that no outside consultant can or should attempt to dictate his client's strategy. No outside consultant can ever learn enough about his client's business nor will he ever know as much about that business as the people who run it. Nor should we attempt to set the strategy if we are not going to have to live with the results of that strategy.

The role that an outside consultant can undertake, however, is to *facilitate* the process of strategic thinking. As facilitators, we can keep the forum on track and bring objectivity to the discussions. We do not use the word facilitator to mean having someone in the room to take notes. Our meaning is that of a *trained* facilitator following a *predetermined process* and using *predesigned instruments* to ensure that all the necessary questions are raised and debated. A facilitator's role is to place the participants in the appropriate discussion groups in order to tap everyone's knowledge and expertise in an orderly way. It is with this understanding of our role that we can then assist clients to set their own direction following a time-efficient formula which we will now describe.

PHASE I: PREWORK

Each member of the management team answers our two questionnaires, the Current Profile Survey and the Strategic Input Analysis Survey.

This work requires three to five hours of effort by each person and is done without consulting their colleagues. Our objective is to extract each person's best thinking on all the key elements of the business and its environment. Their answers are sent to us for editing and collating.

PHASE II: THREE-DAY WORKSESSION

With the sum of views from the two questionnaires as our major inputs we now come together to establish a strategy and a *future* strategic profile. During this session, management discusses all of these inputs in subgroups using predesigned discussion instruments which raise all the necessary questions and activate the debate.

The three days are divided as follows:

Day I

- We obtain agreement on the current profile and the current *driving force*.
- We review all the strategic inputs and agree on the two or three most important ones in each category.

Day II

- We use the abridged strategic inputs to choose two or three potential driving forces.
- We develop profiles for each potential driving force and compare them to the current profile.
- We choose a *tentative strategic profile*.

Day III

- We develop competitive strategic profiles.
- We test the *tentative strategic profile* and surface *critical issues*. We shape and mold the *final strategic profile*.

PHASE III: TWO-DAY WORKSESSION

After a three to four week break, we reassemble for another two days at which time we start addressing and resolving some of the *critical issues*.

During this process, the facilitator compiles, edits, collates, and produces all discussion papers and final reports.

"Three days to set the direction of an organization is not enough time," some people will say. Our answer to that is, "That is true when you don't have a process." Without a process, executives can literally spend months and sometimes years trying to get agreement as to the future direction of the organization. This happens because the lack of methodology forces strategy formulation to be done on-the-run and in a haphazard way. With a good process, three days is more than ample time as we've proven in a large number of client organizations.

Many of the systems that we have seen used in many companies are overly complex and time consuming. Too frequently they end up producing volumes of paper that end up on the bookshelf together with the pictures and the awards.

Our process produces a strategic profile that a person can remember easily and practice daily. When transcribed to paper, it should not be more than two or three pages in length. The most successful organizations are those that keep things simple and do a few things extremely well. The same is true of strategic thinking.

PHASE IV: TWO-DAY REVIEW

Some eight to ten months after the first worksession, we reconvene as a group to revisit our strategy. Because the conclusions of the first three-day session were reached on the basis of assumptions that were made about what might or might not occur in the environment, we now need to reassess those assumptions. This reassessment will also allow us to "fine-tune" our strategic position and surface any new critical issues.

NINE

How Strategic Thinking Is Used in Organizations

In working with our clients we have gained a wealth of experience. This experience has led us to some conclusions as to how a strategic thinking process can best assist the executive of an organization. Although it would be nice to offer a list of do's and don'ts, we have found that the process is universal in its application even though some adaption needs to be done to suit each organization's distinct culture. Instead of listing the ideal circumstances under which a strategic thinking process can bring the best results, we thought it better to share with you our experience to date and that of some of our clients. In many cases they are our own observations; in others, those of our clients.

WHERE DO YOU START?

When we first began to work in this field, our answer to this question was, "You can only start strategic thinking at the top of the organization." Fortunately, the years have made us wiser. Many times this wisdom has come at the insistence of a client who wanted to use the process even though we were not starting at the very top of the corporate structure. Surprisingly, it worked just as well. The conclusion we have drawn, however, is that single-product companies are different from multi-product ones. In a single-product company, strategic thinking originates from a single source—top management. In a multi-product company, however, each division or unit does its own strategic thinking. In such a structure, the process can be used by any unit that has *discretion* over its scope of products, markets, users, and accompanying resources.

Sometimes, someone will ask, "How can we set strategy at the divisional level, when we are not aware of the corporate strategy?" Our experience here shows that managers should not abdicate their obligation to think strategically even though the corporate strategy is not always clear. Some executives have found this process a good tool to explain their rationale to their superiors in order to obtain endorsement for the pursuit of a certain direction at the divisional level. At each level, it is the task of the strategist, the general manager or vice-president, to formulate the best possible strategy for that level that is compatible with what is thought to be the corporate strategy.

Our conclusion: you start where there is a discrete unit and a need for clarity of direction.

HOW LARGE DOES AN ORGANIZATION NEED TO BE?

Size has no relationship to the need to think strategically. We have worked with organizations with billions of dollars of revenue down to a print shop with revenues of about $1,000,000 and eighteen employees. The results are the same.

The key element, rather than size, is the degree of discretion the executives of any unit have over the direction of that unit. If discretion is allowed over the scope of products and markets, then strategic thinking is a requirement and thus applicable at that level.

CASCADING THE PROCESS

Most clients who do start at or close to the top will quickly see the benefits of *cascading* the process down the organization. In fact, this means repeating the exercise in divisions or subunits in order to obtain consensus and commitment at all important levels of management. At the lower levels the process is used more as a tool to get people on a "common-wavelength" in regards to the direction of the organization rather than as a tool to change that direction. Nevertheless, the result can be very effective since having clarity of direction at many levels of management encourages better use of time, effort, and resources.

HOW FAR DOWN DO YOU GO?

Although most of our work is with organizations or subunits of organizations who are looking to set direction for total business units, we have done some work for certain *functions* of corporate entities. For example, we have worked with the R&D and the human resource functions of large multi-national companies. Surprisingly, even functions can have *strategic drive* and many times these are not clearly defined. Is the HRD function product-driven or user/market-driven? This question makes for a very lively debate. The answer chosen will greatly affect the nature of the services offered by HRD and the composition of its staff.

Our suggestion, therefore, is that the process can be cascaded down to the key functions of the company, especially to the functions that have been identified as *areas of excellence*. In these areas, it is imperative that the personnel clearly understand the corporate direction and their role and purpose within that framework.

HOW DO WE LINK THIS INTO OUR OPERATIONAL PLANNING PROCESS?

This is a natural and timely question which arises after each strategic thinking assignment. In our opinion, however, it is wrongly phrased. A better question would be, "How do we link the operational plan into our strategic profile?"

When asked this way, three things will occur within the organization:

1. the timeframe of the operational planning cycle will be revisited and altered to dovetail with the strategic timeframe.
2. the operational planning process will be "cleansed" of its misplaced strategic elements and reissued strictly as an operation (how-to) planning tool.
3. with a clear profile and direction, the operational and strategic plans will be simplified.

The third point is an important one. Due to the lack of a strategic profile, operational planning systems are quite complicated. They have to project *many* scenarios in order to anticipate all conceivable situations. They often seemed based on a dialogue between Alice and the Cheshire Cat in *Alice in Wonderland*.

Alice: Would you tell me, please, which way I ought to go from here?

Cat: That depends a good deal on where you want to get to.

Alice: I don't much care where.

Cat: Then it doesn't matter which way you go!

Many operational planning systems in use today practice what we call "total horizon scenarios." Because of a lack of a clear strategy and strategic profile, people develop plans outlining *all* possible scenarios available to the organization.

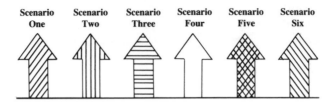

With a clear strategic profile the business plan need contain only a few scenarios—those that will get us there! Strategic thinking allows a rifle shot approach to forward planning rather than a shotgun one. We have never found the concept of "Ready-Fire-Aim" to be favored among CEOs who viewed themselves as good strategists.

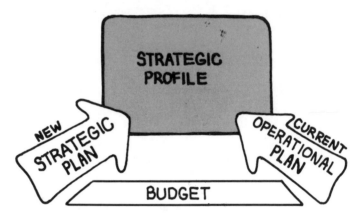

With the direction firmly established, the operational and strategic planning systems can be simplified. Only the budget needs to be added and our planning process is ready for execution.

In this process, the strategic profile is the *rationale* for the business plan. The strategic plan should "scoop up" all *new* product, market, and user opportunities to be pursued. The operational plan should deal with *current* activities. If *new* activities are delegated to managers who are dealing with *current* ones, their likelihood of occurring is lessened as these people are completely engrossed with today's "operational locomotive" and cannot devote time or energy to anything else. The budget should then allow for the necessary resources to accomplish both the strategic and operational plans.

WHEN SHOULD WE REVIEW OUR STRATEGY?

Unlike a business planning or operational planning process which operates like clockwork, there is no set rule as to when the strategic profile should be revisited. Most clients want to do so approximately nine to twelve months after the first exercise. This is usually a quick review to verify any assumptions made previously and to monitor the progress made on the critical issues. After that, review of the strategic profile should be done as indicators in the environment are noticed which threaten the *business concept* of the organization.

Richard T. Pascale of the Stanford Graduate School of Business seems to agree, as illustrated in *Business Week*, "The New Breed of Strategic Planner":

Very often, procedures like the annual strategic planning cycle haven't been terribly effective, partly because strategy doesn't need to be changed every year. Strategy comes to be seen as a rain dance, a fire drill, not to be taken seriously. The process ends up having the perverse effect of desensitizing people to strategic issues. Strategy becomes a routine exercise, rather than something expected of each person each day.

Another instance which may cause a desire to revisit one's strategy is when a feeling develops that it has ended up "somewhere we didn't plan to be." This occurs when the business concept ends up in a marketplace it was not intended for. A recent example was Apple with its original business concept of "a personal computer for the home." Their personal computer, however, ended up being bought by managers and being used as a small *business* computer. However successful Apple has been, one could say it has been by accident and not by design. I suspect that this issue was probably at the root of the conflict between John Sculley and Steven Jobs which caused Jobs' departure. Since then, Sculley has obviously changed Apple's strategy to focus more on the business market. When we end up with products, markets, and users by "accident," then is a good opportunity to review our strategic thinking.

WHAT IS THE ROLE OF THE CHIEF EXECUTIVE?

Most chief executives are not measured by the immediate results they bring to the corporation but rather by the legacy they leave their successors. They are judged by the clarity or confusion of direction they leave behind.

The head of any unit that wishes to set the direction of that organization must take an active and leading role in the strategic thinking process. The process provided him with an opportunity to take inventory of his people's best thinking as well as a forum to explain his own views. It is by participating in the process itself that the chief executive places his "imprint" on the future direction of the organization.

WHAT IS THE ROLE OF LINE MANAGERS AND PLANNING STAFF?

The only people who must formulate and implement strategy are the chief executive and senior line management. These are the "stakeholders" in the organization's future direction since it is this group that will live with the results of that choice. It is imperative, then, that these people participate fully in the process so that their views and opinions are aired and discussed.

A tragedy of North American business in the 1970s has been the abdication by line executives of their role as *formulators* and *implementors* of strategy. Many senior executives have passed on their obligation as chief architects of strategy to corporate planning staff and, as a result, much of the forward thinking of the 1970s was being done by a burgeoning bureaucracy of "corporate" planners or "strategic" planners using complex models which, for the most part, forgot to include the most important component of forward thinking—the human touch. Most "planning" systems do not allow for the ingenuity, creativity, innovativeness, resiliency, versatility, power, and dynamism of the human mind. Nor do they consider the values, beliefs, or principles of these people, another element that shapes the scope of products and markets in every organization.

Corporate planners are very often very skilled people but their role should not be as formulators or implementors of strategy. They can play a vital role as collectors, evaluators, assessors, and monitors of vital information needed for forward thinking but since they, like outside consultants, do not have to live with the results, their role must support and complement line management but not replace it. Too much reliance on "a" system of forward thinking or planning usually results in a static method of planning and a "not-invented-here" syndrome. The most successful corporate planners are those which act as "brokers" between senior management and the outside world. They act as the "eyes" of top management to scan the outside world for tools and outside organizations that can assist management achieve their goals.

WHAT IS THE ROLE OF THE FACILITATOR?

The question of using external or internal resources as facilitators of the process is an important one and usually comes up in all large companies with whom we work.

Normally, most clients will ask us to facilitate the initial interventions. As the desire to cascade the process down the organization increases, then it makes sense for the client to use internal resources. One part of our service is then to train these internal facilitators and equip them to continue the effort within their respective units. There are a number of good reasons to do this.

• The client, or user, takes ownership of the process.
• Internal facilitators can assist in the management of critical issues.

- Internal facilitators can "tailor" the instruments to unique or different situations.
- Internal facilitators can assist with the integration of the operational and strategic plans into the strategic profile.

THE RESULTS

We have noticed a variety of different results from the use of this process and we make a point of asking each of our clients what value they received. Without exception, six items are always mentioned.

Clarity

Although not every client changes his direction as a result of this exercise, every client has said that the process brought *clarity* to their strategic thinking. As a group the management team start the process with slightly different perceptions of the company's strategy or, in some instances, with a non-articulated and somewhat fuzzy strategy. At the end of the exercise, however, they have produced a crystal-clear strategic profile. Each member of the management team now shares only *one* vision of the organization's future.

The profile can also be used to bring clarity to other people in the organization. Some of our clients have published parts or all of the strategic profile to communicate the company's strategy to various interested groups including annual reports to inform shareholders of the company's direction. Others have used it as a discussion piece in internal forums with employees.

Corporate beliefs usually get published extensively. As the *driving force* is the heart of strategic thinking, corporate beliefs are its *soul*.

Focus

Focus is another output of the process. The strategic profile produces a better tool to allocate resources and to manage the time and efforts of others. It enables them to direct their efforts toward activities that complement the desired direction of the company and to avoid wasted efforts on non-related issues.

When we asked the chief executive of Alcan why the metal tent card with the words "Our product is aluminum" faces the visitor to his office, he replied, "I don't want any of our people talking to me about any other subject than aluminum."

Consensus

The process brings about consensus at each step. The debates and discussions are conducted in such a manner that agreement is achieved *systematically* on each key issue before moving on the next one. The assignments worked on during the worksession are designed to place on the table all the key questions about the future of the organization. These instruments bring forward everyone's best thinking and provide an opportunity for each person to present his views, opinions, and rationale on each important issue. We have found that it is not sufficient only to collect a person's perceptions through a survey, but that a person needs an opportunity to explain and elaborate his point of view.

A group vice-president said of his superior, the sector vice president, at the end of one of our worksessions, "I have worked with this man for over 20 years. Yet, I found out more about his views on our business in the last 3 days." This expression has been heard in many of the strategy sessions we have been involved with.

Because the process provides a forum to discuss these issues in an orderly manner, there is never a dissenting voice at the end of the worksession. This unquestionably contributes to a more harmonious organization.

Cohesion

"Hockey-stick planning," one executive told us, "leads to hockey-puck management." Without a clear strategic profile the organization bounces from one seemingly good idea to another. It zig-zags its way forward and expends valuable time, money, and effort leap-frogging from one suspicious opportunity to another. When there is no clear direction accompanied by a solid *test-bed* to screen opportunities, management can often be seduced by the financial aspects of that opportunity only to discover later that there is no fit with the rest of their activities. The strategic profile becomes the bedrock or cornerstone of their actions and, when used in such a manner, results in a synchronization of resources instead of dispersion and fragmentation. Less time will be wasted exploring undesired options and less effort will be expended justifying the existence of the "sunset" portions of the business.

Commitment

There is absolute commitment from each management team member to the new direction. The reason is simple: it is *their* strategy. They participated at every step. All their views were heard and their inputs considered. This commitment sometimes comes from surprising quarters. The vice-president of a division of a complex multinational, whose unit was going to be de-emphasized in the future, said to us, "I recognize the fact that we're not going to be getting the same resources as in the past, but I'm totally committed to that decision. I now understand why those funds need to be given to other parts of the business." This is an important achievement. Every organization must discriminate between its various units when allocating resources, and it is important that the managers of the less fortunate units understand the reasons. These units still need to be managed well even though they may not be the "stars" of the future. In this instance our process served as a unifying force within that organization.

"For any strategy to succeed, you need oprating people to *understand* it, *embrace* it, and *make it happen*," says Roger Schipke, Senior Vice President of General Electric. We couldn't agree more.

Filter

Probably the best use of the strategic profile is that of a filter for the operational plans and new product or market opportunities.

As an operational filter, it can reduce and even eliminate "hockey-puck" management. The strategic profile clearly identifies the areas of *more* emphasis and *less* emphasis in the future. This knowledge should be "etched" on the brain of every key manager and used as a "working sieve to guide their daily operational decisions and actions." Such was the use a general manager of a client organization wanted his subordinates to make of this tool.

More important, however, the strategic profile is an excellent way to ferret out good from less promising products or market opportunities.

When these opportunities present themselves, a few questions can quickly test their "fit" with our strategic profile and direction.

"Does this opportunity complement or violate the *driving force* and *business concept*?"

"Does this opportunity bring products that fit those which will receive more emphasis or less emphasis in the future?"

"Does this opportunity bring markets that fit those which will receive more emphasis or less emphasis in the future?"

"Does the opportunity bring users that fit those which will receive more emphasis or less emphasis in the future?"

"Does this opportunity bring products, markets, and users which can be supported by the present areas of excellence? Or will they require excellence in other areas beyond our current capabilities?"

"Does this opportunity meet the size/growth, return/profit guidelines?"

This quick test can help an organization in two ways:

1. If you receive negative responses to each of these questions—beware, it might be a good financial opportunity but there might not be an appropriate "fit" with what you are currently doing. Experience has shown that there needs to be more reason than money to wish to exploit an opportunity. In our view those other reasons are a fit with the driving force, business concept, areas of excellence, and product, market, and user scopes.
2. If there is no apparent fit, but you still want to pursue the opportunity, then it might be better to do so under some other form of organization structure. Your present structure does not support the type of opportunity being considered. Another form might.

It is when used in this manner that the strategic profile serves as a framework for day-to-day decisions.

The value that a *strategic thinking* process brings to a company is hard to measure in tangible terms. We have been involved with clients that have made important strategic decisions during the worksession which involved substantial sums of money and which had enormous impact on the company. The intangible rewards, however, are much more discrete but probably have as much of an impact. These seem to be of as much value to clients as the more tangible ones.

TEN

Strategic Management

"No strategy will be effective regardless of how beautifully written it is if its business is conducted as a series of independent transactions. An executive who manages by transaction may be considered to be a shrewd operator, a good trader, or a good deal maker, but he is not managing strategically." So says William C. Waddell in *The Outline of Strategy*.

Successful CEOs must effectively manage both the "what" and the "how." In other words, strategic management is having a well-thought-out *strategy* which will give the organization a sustainable competitive advantage over time while *operationally* executing that strategy daily to produce desired levels of profit. Both are interrelated. However, our suggestion is that operational effectiveness without sound strategic thinking is doomed to failure. Philip Kotler, in his latest book, *The New Competition*, alluded to this notion.

Any firm must therefore fight today's competitive battles at the same time that it is preparing for the battles of tomorrow. Unless the seeds of future successes are sown today, success in the current and imminent battles may prove to be pyrrhic victories—the battles are won but the war is lost.

The key to strategic management then, is how to manage the business well operationally while at the same time positioning it strategically to maintain, sustain, and improve its competitive and strategic edge.

At this point in any strategic project, the issue that surfaces within a client organization is, "How do we manage strategically on an ongoing basis?"

Obviously this is a key question that begs an answer if the strategic thinking process is to be institutionalized within the organization.

Our experience to date shows that management must pay attention to five activities in order to institutionalize this process. Let's look at each one separately.

ORGANIZATION STRUCTURE

We trained hard . . . but it seemed that every time we were beginning to form up into teams we would be reorganized. I was to realize later in life that we tend to meet any new situation by reorganizing; and a wonderful method it can be for creating the illusion of progress while providing confusion, inefficiency and demoralization.

Petronius Arbiter 210 B.C.

Many corporations went through a stage, in the late 60s and early 70s, of reorganization. Reorganizing, back then, seemed to be a favorite pastime. One of the favorite organization models used during this period was the matrix model. Once reorganized, then the question was asked, "Where do we go from here?"

Our position is very clear. *The organization structure should support the strategic profile and not vice-versa.*

Again, our work shows that there is no ideal organization form. The key element is the driving force. A technology-driven company should not be structured like a user/market–driven company. Each one's corporate behaviour is different and the structure should reflect this. The structure of each should be such that it supports and promotes the direction of the corporate entity.

PRODUCT/SERVICE-DRIVEN ORGANIZATION

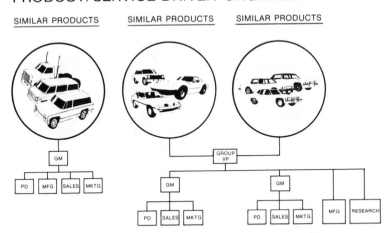

SIMILAR PRODUCTS   SIMILAR PRODUCTS   SIMILAR PRODUCTS

USER/MARKET NEEDS-DRIVEN ORGANIZATION

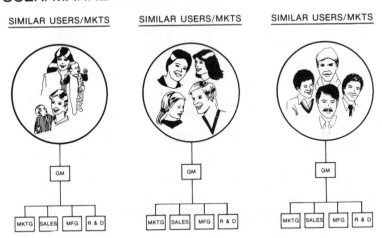

SIMILAR USERS/MKTS   SIMILAR USERS/MKTS   SIMILAR USERS/MKTS

TECHNOLOGY-DRIVEN ORGANIZATION

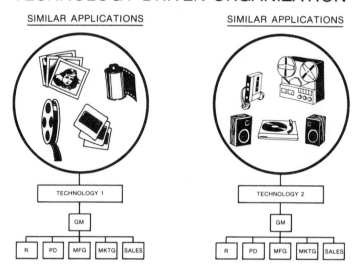

SIMILAR APPLICATIONS   SIMILAR APPLICATIONS

TECHNOLOGY 1   TECHNOLOGY 2

GM   GM

R | PD | MFG | MKTG | SALES   R | PD | MFG | MKTG | SALES

RETURN/PROFIT DRIVEN ORGANIZATION

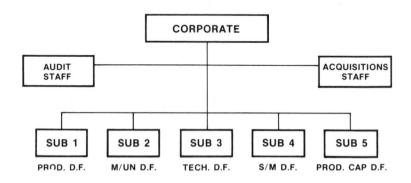

CORPORATE

AUDIT STAFF   ACQUISITIONS STAFF

SUB 1 | SUB 2 | SUB 3 | SUB 4 | SUB 5

PROD. D.F.   M/UN D.F.   TECH. D.F.   S/M D.F.   PROD. CAP D.F.

STRATEGIC BUSINESS UNITS (SBUs)

Another fad of the 70s was the strategic business unit. Many corporations set up profit centers as SBUs, when in fact, they were strictly operating units. What is the dividing line between an operating unit and an SBU?

To us, the distinction is clear and simple. A strategic business unit is one whose management has discretion over the nature of products offered and markets sought. Discretion does not mean they do things without approval, but it does mean that they can make recommendations and take decisions that can alter the "look" of their products and markets. These are *true* strategic units. Other units which do not have this discretion or whose task it is to implement a higher management level's choice of products and markets is only an operating unit and not a strategic one.

As mentioned before, the full strategic thinking process can be applied equally as well at the SBU level as the corporate level. For operating units, on the other hand, our process incorporates *contribution statements*. These are mini-profiles which clarify the purpose, the role, and the contribution each operating unit is expected to make toward the realization of the corporate strategic profile.

Knowing when and how to change the configuration of business units becomes a key activity of strategic management. Once again we revert back to the concept of driving force. The structure of strategic business units should be reviewed as we detect changes in their driving forces. A key indicator for the need to restructure is when we see overlaps of products and markets between SBUs. This overlap is caused by overlapping driving forces. Our SBU network should be constructed in a manner to bring out the synergy between the various driving forces.

INFORMATION SYSTEMS—MONITORING THE ENVIRONMENT

One frequently hears the statement that corporate survival means "monitoring the environment for impending changes." The environment in which most corporations operate is a vast one. No organization can monitor *everything* in its environment. Too often we have seen environmental data that ends up costing substantially more than its value as a tool of strategic management.

The elements that must be monitored carefully are those variables that could weaken or strengthen our driving force. Thus, the *areas of excellence* which give our *driving force* its strength are the elements that need careful and ongoing surveillance in order to manage the corporation's destiny. The corporate *areas of excellence* will be the areas that outside forces will try to attack.

We mentioned earlier that Exxon was natural resources–driven. What better way to reduce the strength of Exxon than by cutting off its access to those resources. Nationalization is any oil company's most serious threat because it attacks their "raison d'être" as an organization and threatens to cut off its lifeline.

Different *driving forces* will induce us to monitor different elements of the environment. A technology-driven company will want to be on the lookout for any breakthroughs that might make its technology obsolete. As a result, they will usually attend, and even organize, symposia where such information is shared. It is also a subscriber to many scientific journals in order to monitor very carefully the scientific and technical environment.

A user/market–driven company will spend a lot of time talking to its users to detect early any signs of dissatisfaction and to monitor changing habits and demographics.

A product/service–driven company will keep a watchful eye on the competition. It buys their products and regularly does side-by-side comparisons to evaluate their performance, seeking to close gaps as quickly as possible.

A production capacity/capability–driven company will spend its time at industry trade shows where new equipment is exhibited. They are looking for ways and means of making their own equipment faster and better in order to lower unit cost.

A profit/return–driven company will spend must of its time monitoring itself. Each unit's performance is closely audited to insure financial performance and to detect early any deviations from these goals. Units that miss these goals frequently are quickly sold.

COMMITTEES

Most organizations have committees in place whose role is to facilitate the decision making within the organization. An important element of strategic management is to ensure that strategic thinking is an ongoing activity and not seen as an extra responsibility and burden to the management team.

To this end, agendas for these committees should be separated between *strategic issues* and *operational issues*. The strategic issues are naturally the critical issues. Some organizations have gone as far as establishing a strategic management committee to review the progress made on the critical issues. The members of this committee are those that have a vital stake in shaping the profile and future of the organization.

FOCUS MANAGEMENT

One of our pet suggestions to management after a strategic thinking session is to adopt a management style and attitude that we call *Focus Management*. Basically, the concept is simple. Focus on the important issues and manage those well because one can't do everything. The issues that are important to the future of the organization are the critical issues. If the *future strategic profile* is to materialize, these are the issues that need to be resolved. Lack of action on these issues will not bring about any change of direction.

Even General Electric is moving away from the portfolio matrix system of strategic planning to an *issue-oriented* approach. William E. Rothschild, a planner on G.E.'s corporate staff, observed, "We're spending time to get people to attack where there are business opportunities rather than saying let's start over on every business every year. Our effort will be built more around specific issues and less on specific businesses."

To assure action on the critical issues, several things need to be done:

1. Because there may be several issues, a priority needs to be assigned to each issue.

2. The *result expected* for each issue is identified in advance as a clear target for the owner.

3. Next, each issue must be assigned an *owner*. This is the person who will undertake the task of seeing that issue resolved. When there is no clear ownership of an issue, it will fall between the slots and disappear.

4. Contributors—people who can assist the owner with the resolution—are identified for each issue.

5. An action plan is put into place for each issue.

6. Completion dates are set.

7. A *review date* to monitor progress is established.

One of the most difficult aspects of strategic management occurs when there is a change of direction. In such an instance, the most difficult elements to manage in the implementation of a new strategy are not the "hard" issues such as technology, products, markets, distribution system, and so forth, but rather the "soft" issues such as corporate culture, image, people profiles, and compensation.

FOCUS MANAGEMENT
CRITICAL ISSUES

ISSUE	PRIORITY	OWNER	CONTRIBUTORS	RESULT EXPECTED	REVIEW DATE
1. ~~~~~ ~~~~~	HIGH	H. SMITH	JIM, JOE, PAUL	~~~~~ ~~~~~	QTR 1
2. ~~~~~ ~~~~~	HIGH	J. DRAKE	HARRY, MARY	~~~~~ ~~~~~	1/9
3. ~~~~~ ~~~~~	HIGH	B. LEIGH	JIM, Q.C.	~~~~~ ~~~~~	10/2
4. ~~~~~ ~~~~~	HIGH	J. BROWN	MGNT COMMITEE	~~~~~ ~~~~~	QTR 3
5. ~~~~~ ~~~~~	MEDIUM	P. BURNS	ENRG./R & D	~~~~~ ~~~~~	ON-GOING

Over a period of time every organization develops a corporate "mindset" that reflects the strategy or business concept it is pursuing. This mindset is seen in the types of people it recruits, the compensation system, and the road to success within the corporation. Because the *driving force* of an organization maintains its strength by excellence in certain areas of activity, a change of *strategic drive* will bring with it a need to change the areas of excellence. This, in turn, may require changes in the corporate value system.

The road to success in a product-driven organization is through the sales force and sales management. Chief Executives usually were top sales people previously. In a market/user–driven organization, the road to success is through the marketing arm. In a technology-driven organization, it is engineers and scientists who migrate to the top while accountants succeed in return/profit–driven companies. In view of this, the reward system is usually geared accordingly. Sales people make more money, gain more prestige, and generally are the most revered group of people in a product-driven organization. In market/user–driven organizations that treatment is reserved for the marketing wizards.

A key critical issue to manage during the transition from one area of *strategic drive* to another are the "soft" issues such as areas of excellence, reward systems, corporate culture, and the status and image of people within the organization. Any change of direction will change the winners and losers within the organization and the proper management of the ensuant "people" issues will probably determine the success or failure of that strategy.

Focus Management means the management of critical issues. It entails the delegation of these to the responsible people and the monitoring of progress made. It also means the deletion of resolved issues and the addition of new issues as these surface.

Focus Management ensures that management's attention is riveted to the *right* issues which shape the future direction of the organization. This allows them to manage *proactively* the implications that any change in strategy always brings rather than to deal with these after-the-fact from a *reactive* position.

ELEVEN

Using Strategic Thinking for Competitive Advantage

As mentioned in a previous chapter, a proactive strategy is one that allows you to control or influence the rules of play in the competitive sandbox. Some experts will tell you that the way to do this is to do an analysis of each competitor's strengths and weaknesses and then to exploit those weaknesses. Time and again, while working in strategy sessions with successful CEOs, this was not usually of great appeal to them. When asked "Why not?" one CEO replied, "I'm not interested in spending *my* money to make any competitor stronger." When asked to clarify this statement, he went on to explain that attacking a competitor's weakness makes the competitor recognize this weakness and then do things to correct or eliminate it. You have awakened the competitor to that weakness, gained a competitive edge temporarily, but then given that competitor a long-term advantage. You now need to attack another weakness and the whole cycle starts over. If you carry this scenario to its logical but somewhat absurd end, eventually you will have strengthened that competitor so much that he might put you out of business.

A better way, in our opinion, to deal with competitors is to anticipate each competitor's *strategy* and then manage *their* strategy which will put you in a *proactive* position while they will be kept in a *reactive* one. The steps to do this are as follows.

WHICH COMPETITORS WILL YOUR STRATEGY ATTRACT?

Once your own strategy has been developed, look around to see which organizations will be attracted to such a strategy. If your strategy represents a change from the one you have pursued in the past, the competitors it will attract will not be the same as your past competitors.

ANTICIPATE EACH POTENTIAL COMPETITOR'S FUTURE STRATEGY

The next step is to anticipate each competitor's *business strategy*. At this point, some might say that that cannot be done since we do not sit in on the competitor's strategy sessions. However, the strategy of any company ends up translating itself into physical evidence such as products, geographic markets, customers, buildings, technologies, facilities, people, skills, and so forth. By looking at the actions of a competitor in these areas one can identify what drove the competitor to do that. In other words, what was the *driving force* behind that competitor's strategy. In the same manner, by looking at a competitor's current actions, announced actions, or anticipated actions, we can identify the *driving force* of that competitor's *future* strategy. This can be done for each competitor that you think your strategy will attract.

DRAW COMPETITIVE PROFILES

You can now anticipate where each competitor will put its emphasis and de-emphasis in terms of products, users, and geographic markets. You can now draw "pictures" of what each competitor will look like from the pursuit of such a strategy. One misconception exists, however, about competitive behavior. Many people assume that all the competitors in one industry behave the same way. Not necessarily so. Usually, each competitor's *driving force* or *strategic drive* is different and will act differently under a similar set of circumstances. However, if you detect each competitor's *driving force*, you can also anticipate each one's behaviour and then you can put into place a different set of actions to deal with each competitor differently.

MANAGE THE COMPETITOR'S STRATEGY

Not so long ago, we had the opportunity to work with one of the best known manufacturers of buses. When we arrived at this stage in the process, one competitor was identified to be pursuing a "copy cat" strategy. In other words, whatever bus contract our client bid upon, a few weeks later that competitor would enter a similar bid but at a lower price. If our client chose not to bid, neither would the competitor. This pattern repeated itself all over the world. Once this competitor's strategy was recognized, a plan was developed to "manage" that competitor's strategy. A very large project emerged involving some four thousand buses. Because of previous bad experience in that part of the world, our client did not want this project. However, to lure the competitor, the company put in a bid which included more services than required and at a price well below cost. Sure enough, the competitor bid and was awarded the project. Two-thirds of the way into the project that competitor ran into major cost overruns to the extent that the company recently announced it is looking for a merger partner to help it out of its financial difficulties.

CONTROL THE COMPETITIVE SANDBOX

Control the sandbox. If your strategy is to be proactive, it must enable you to control or at least influence the rules of play in the competitive sandbox. This, as mentioned earlier, is not achieved by attacking a competitor's weakness. You do not achieve this either, by attacking a competitor's many strengths. Managing a competitor's strategy and controlling the sandbox can only be achieved by attacking a competitor's *areas of excellence*. As described in a previous chapter, the strategy of any company is supported by the development of expertise or skills in a couple of key strategic areas and it is these *areas of excellence* that make that company's strategy work. Therefore, the same concept applies in reverse. If you want to weaken a competitor's strategy, attack that competitor's areas of excellence. Diluting, diminishing, or possibly eliminating those areas of excellence is the best way in which you can obtain a significant advantage and control or influence the sandbox. You attack the heart and guts of the business. You attack the *driving force* and *areas of excellence* of that competitor. You go for the throat. There is no such thing as genteel competition. The Japanese attacked at the heart of American automobile companies' businesses—they made better cars!

McGowan of MCI did exactly the same against AT&T. AT&T's *driving force* was its distribution system—its network. MCI attacked at the heart of AT&T's business on two fronts. One, in the law courts to break AT&T's legal monopoly, and a second action in the marketplace with the use of a microwave distribution system to bypass and replace the copper wire system of AT&T. By going for the "throat" a small, insignificant company only ten years ago has become a major player in the telecommunications field. On the other, AT&T which controlled the sandbox then, has not yet recovered from that shock and for several years after its breakup, AT&T did not have a coherent reactive strategy in place, much less a proactive one.

Back in 1978, Bell Canada (no relationship to AT&T) faced the same threats AT&T did. Its executive committee reacted in a much different manner. Using the process described in this book and in strategy sessions facilitated by this author, Bell Canada developed a very different strategy to deal with those threats. Today, Bell Canada is still *one* company and is Canada's largest company. The strategy developed and implemented in those sessions has been so successful that it generated enough excess profit to allow it to be a major shareholder in a number of other businesses *without* losing a single piece of its telephone business and *without* having MCI, IBM, or others as major competitors. In fact, in Canada, MCI and IBM are customers of Bell Canada. With a little bit of *strategic thinking* AT&T could have done the same thing.

Digital Equipment Corp. has recently made some impressive gains against IBM. DEC did not do this by only going after IBM's weaknesses. It attacked, as *Business Week* recently reported, in "IBM–DEC Wars," "IBM's best markets—large financial service companies and corporate data processing centers." And DEC is winning.

Once you have identified your competitor's future *driving force* and translated it into a profile of products, markets, and customers that will result from that strategy, you now need to identify the *areas of excellence* that each competitor is cultivating to support that strategy. These will be different from one competitor to another since each is probably pursuing a different strategy. Once this has been done, you are now ready to proceed to the step of determining *which* sandbox you want to play in.

CHOOSE YOUR COMPETITORS, DON'T LET COMPETITORS CHOOSE YOU

Each company, to be proactive, must *consciously* choose which competitive arena it wants to be in. All successful CEOs we have worked with were always careful not to be drawn into competitive arenas by *mistake*. In order to choose *your* sandbox and control the terms of play, two decisions now must be made. From the previous step you can choose your competitors. The first class of competitors you should include in your sandbox are those whose *areas of excellence* you *think* you can successfully attack. Forget the others. If you don't disturb them, they probably will not disturb you. The second class of competitors to include in your sandbox are those that are in a position of attacking *your areas of excellence*. These you want to watch very carefully. It is these competitors or potential competitors that could give your strategy difficulty. The rest of the competitors who are not in a position to attack the guts of your business will be headaches periodically but are not likely to affect your strategy dramatically. If anything, they will attack your weaknesses and give you a chance to strengthen yourself. Competitive tactics will take care of this bunch. It is the competitors who can make your *areas of excellence* and *driving force* obsolete that are much more worrisome. These are, strategically, much more important to you.

STRATEGY ASSESSMENT

Competitive advantage, however, is only one element of business strategy. A number of other questions need to be asked periodically in an ongoing attempt to assess the effectiveness of your overall *business* strategy.

The following are questions that can help a CEO assess the strength or weakness of his/her current strategy.

- Is there growth left in the strategy?

    A strategy that cannot produce growth equal to or better than GNP or population growth will probably not produce enough profits to fuel itself. A new strategy should be explored.

- What is the balance between internal and external opportunities for our strategy?

    A strategy that is completely dependent on internally generated opportunities will probably start sputtering after a while. A good strategy must bring with it an excess of external opportunities to find long-term growth and the chance to uncover new businesses outside the current ones.

- What is the balance between external opportunities and external threats for our strategy?

    If the strategy is faced with a greater number of, and more severe, external threats than opportunities, this is a signal to review the strategy.

- Is there something in the external environment that could make our strategy obsolete?

    If the answer is "yes" or even "probably," there is an urgent need for a strategy review.

- Does our strategy play off our strengths or does it require us to correct some weaknesses?

    A good strategy should allow you to build and improve your strategic strengths. A strategy that forces you to correct weaknesses while not adding to your strengths will not be as effective in the medium-term.

- Is there any competitive activity that might invalidate our strategy?

    Again, a "yes" to this question should trigger a review of the strategy.

The *strategic thinking* process is a tool to develop your own strategy but it is also a tool to help you identify the strategy of your key competitors. Using the *strategic thinking* process in reverse, so to speak, or as if you were in your "competitor's shoes" is a powerful tool to help you "manage" that competitor's strategy.

TWELVE

Strategy in Owner-Managed Companies

One of the privileges we have had over the years is the opportunity to have worked with a wide cross-section of corporations around the world. We have clients in all types of industries and fields from giant multi-nationals to fast-growing medium-sized businesses to small, emerging companies worldwide.

One type of company that caught our attention is the owner-run one. These companies drew our attention because they usually perform better than the large, international giants against which they compete. The reason is simple; they are better managed. In spite of the resources available to large companies, the training it gives to its people, and the expertise it can hire, the fact remains that owner-run companies are better managed. Proof of this conclusion is the recent emergence of the American Business Conference, an association of mid-size high-growth companies whose annual revenue growth must be at least 18% per year, earnings growth of 20% per year, and this for a minimum of five years. This is incredible growth since it means doubling in size every five years. Yet these companies are achieving such levels of growth.

Many of these companies are this successful in spite of the fact that they are going toe-to-toe with some of America's "best managed companies" and, in several cases, even against the best Japanese companies. And they are winning!

The overwhelming majority of these companies are owner-run or have senior executives with substantial equity. Another observation we made while working with CEOs of such organizations is that these CEOs are *better strategists*. They are masters at strategic thinking although they practice it by osmosis.

To all the owner-CEOs we have worked with, strategy is a subject more important to them than their counterparts in non-owner run corporations, including the largest multi-nationals. To owner-CEOs, strategy is a passion! And it is a passion for a number of reasons.

One reason is that they cannot afford mistakes. Large corporations can easily "bury" multi-million dollar mistakes and no one notices. Owner-run companies cannot. As a result, these CEOs are extremely concerned that their strategy is understood by everyone. They also want their people involved in the process for the sake of clarity, consensus, and commitment.

Second, they are concerned about their legacy and perpetuating the organization after their departure. Building a successful organization that can outlive them is a major objective. This is not always the case in large public organizations. One such CEO told us, "Think three years out? Let the next guy worry about that !" Many CEOs who have worked hard for many years for the firm see the CEO's chair as their final "resting place," one they feel they greatly deserve but from which they do not want to make waves. William Shanklin, in a *Planning Review* article, came to a similar conclusion: "the age of the typical CEO is normally 57 when he assumes the position, and then he retires in seven or eight years. This relatively brief tenure encourages a defensive 'don't rock the boat' approach to shepherding a company."

Worrying about their legacy and having a well-articulated strategy is not a strength of the CEOs of publicly-owned corporations. In spite of his success while at ITT, even Harold Geneen was not able to leave in place a strategy that his successor understood or could perpetuate.

We have identified a number of other traits in publicly-owned corporations. Few CEOs are willing to make hard strategic decisions. Their compensation is geared to the value of the stock and this limits their ability to think in the best interests of the corporation and shareholders in the longer run.

Very few have the gumption to do what Ken Olsen of Digital did a few years ago—a corporate restructure and redirection of product development and marketing that included two unprofitable quarters in exchange for a stronger company in the medium and longer term. Or what Akio Morita did in 1980 when he saw Sony's position weakening—accepting no profits for two years and pouring that money into R&D instead—the engine of Sony's long series of innovative new products. It is no coincidence that both these men are owner-CEOs. John Reed, of Citicorp, is presently accepting lower quarterly earnings for a stronger strategic position for his company in the longer term—a bold strategy. John Reed, on the other hand, is in his early forties and probably expects to be around then.

Furthermore, many CEOs in U.S. publicly-owned companies inherited their positions as a result of being in the corporate pecking order. When they end up in the top position, they have no real authority over others in that hierarchy. Many are also not men of vision. Their promotion was due more to being good operational firefighters than strong strategic thinkers. If they have a vision, they have great difficulty communicating it to others. If James Dutt had a vision for Beatrice, not many around him knew or understood it.

As placebos for the lack of a clear strategy, they turn to annual themes— "the Year of Productivity," "the Year of the Customer," or "the Year of Innovation." Or worse, they let their divisions drive corporate strategy by encouraging division general managers to develop their own plans. By encouraging division managers to fight for resources, they assume that only the best plans will prevail and that this is best for the overall performance of the corporations. This is not strategic leadership . . . it is management by default. Milton Lauenstein, of Northeastern University, has the same view.

Unfortunately, many U.S. companies have no strategy worthy of the name. They pursue patterns of actions such as diversification, vertical integration, or market share because they are widely accepted as sound.

Or else they articulate their so-called strategy in "motherhood" statements that allow everyone to nod in approval to but which no one understands in a manner to allow effective implementation. Here's a statement that was arrived at by one of America's largest companies after a four-day meeting of its top twenty-four managers: "Our strategy is to grow our core businesses while we seek new opportunities for growth in other areas globally." How can such a vague and general statement serve lower-level managers as a framework for their decisions as to which products, markets, and customers to pursue and not pursue? Almost anything will fit. Needless to say, this statement of strategy was not the result of our process.

Some CEOs will tell you that their hands are tied by Wall Street and that the U.S. financial system works against thinking strategically. The CEO of a well-known U.S. corporation recently wrote in *Business Week* ("The New Breed of Strategic Planner"),

Wall Street's preoccupation with quarterly earnings has combined to make maximizing shareholder value the primary mandate of many U.S. corporations. Unfortunately, shareholder value is almost entirely equated with short-term stock prices. By this yardstick, the higher the stock price, the better management has done its job. This forces management to put short-term earnings growth before such interests as market development, and customer and employee satisfaction. These are interests that help ensure the long-term success of a company.

This CEO is correct in his observation that Wall Street wants results. But that is but one hypothesis for the lack of strategic thinking in U.S. corporations. Many CEOs of public corporations think that an increase in quarterly performance *is* the strategy of the corporation. They look to increase shareholder value moment-by-moment, quarter-by-quarter even at the loss of corporate strategic position, competitiveness, thrust, and edge. Shareholder value is best improved by the long-term improvement of strategic position in products, skills, productivity and expertise, areas that competitors cannot easily duplicate. Surely, Wall Street is interested in the long-term health of their investments. No mutual fund manager likes to change his investments every quarter. Too often American companies have strayed into acquiring businesses, for the sake of earnings growth, in areas where they have little or no competence. And it is diversification for the sake of earnings growth that has given birth to the "corporate raider."

Dr. Edwin Land, retired founder of Polaroid recently told *Forbes*, ("The Vindication of Edwin Land") of his delight in seeing the current management return the company to its original area of strength—instant photography—with the launch of its new camera, the Spectra. This has occurred after several failed attempts at other, unrelated businesses. Dr. Land's comments:

They [Polaroid's managers] were responding to the pressure of the financial world. But the essence of business leadership in America is to be able to turn your back on the demands of the financial world. Its analyses are never profound.

Leveraged buy-outs (LBOs) are a good example of what can happen to a company when senior executives have a substantial percentage of the equity. Many of these organizations have a dramatic increase in value once you have in place a management team that has its own personal money at stake. Witness the turnaround in value of Beatrice Foods and Metromedia after LBOs. "You are no longer dealing with the same culture, the economic incentives are much more compelling; there is a much higher energy level, a much greater devotion to efficiency and risk-taking," says Alan Rappaport, a specialist in mergers and acquisitions at Northwestern University's Kellogg School of Management.

In owner-run companies, earnings, profit, and market share are the results of strategy . . . not its objective. Profits and market share tell you how well your strategy is working. CEOs of owner-run companies know that shareholder value is best improved in the long-term by continuously improving the firm's strategic position in the *areas it knows the best*. These are the areas that will be difficult for competitors to acquire or duplicate.

They know that constant attention to these key areas is what produces a constant stream of healthy profits.

Another item of proof for these observations lies with the Japanese. The most successful Japanese companies of the last twenty years are those still managed by their *founders*. Morita of Sony, Honda of Honda, the Toyoda family of Toyota, to name but a few. These Japanese owners are in firm command of their strategy and are still pursuing it with singularity of dedication and purpose. On the other hand, many U.S. companies that were built by men such as DuPont, Sloan, Firestone, McKnight, Rockefeller, Ford, Goodyear and others have passed into the hands of professional managers who probably are caught in the situation described by the CEO who wrote the *Business Week* article.

However, even well-intentioned CEOs can sometimes lose sight of the founder's vision. General Motors is a good example. Alfred Sloan's strategy and business concept was simple—" a car for every income strata." Mr. Sloan even articulated his product-driven concept quite clearly—"Each line of General Motors cars produced should preserve a distinction of appearance, so that one knows on sight a Chevrolet, a Pontiac, an Oldsmobile, a Buick or a Cadillac." The concept being that, as a family moved up in income, it could afford a slightly more expensive GM automobile. As a result, GM cars were built to look differently so that they could be priced to appeal to different income levels. In the 70s, GM executives lost sight of this business concept. In an attempt to match the Japanese's manufacturing excellence, they sought production efficiencies by designing their cars alike. The "look alike" strategy totally confused the customers and killed what had been, and still could be, a very successful strategy. In an attempt to gain operational effectiveness, GM executives forfeited their basic strategy.

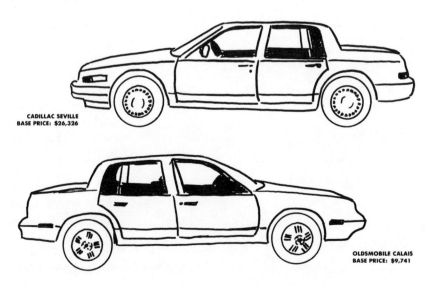

CADILLAC SEVILLE
BASE PRICE: $26,326

OLDSMOBILE CALAIS
BASE PRICE: $9,741

In owner-run companies, on the other hand, the CEO has a firm grasp on the strategy, what *strategic area* drives it, and what the corporation's areas of excellence are that successfully perpetuate that strategy. The CEO views himself as the *strategist* for the organization and the strategy must be his regardless of whose ideas were used. Witness a recent statement by Horace McDonnell, CEO of Perkin-Elmer, one of America's fastest growing computer companies (Hamermesh, *Making Strategy Work*).

We are a technology-driven company. The key to our success has been to invest in many high-technology areas at the same time in order to get some big winners, rather than to ration our efforts. And in high technology, it is *R&D* and *marketing* [areas of excellence], not capital items, that are your key investments.

Although Perkin-Elmer is not one of our clients, McDonnell is obviously a good strategist and a conscious practitioner of the concepts and process described in this book which, as stated before, were developed by watching such CEOs in the exercise of developing and managing strategy.

THIRTEEN

Applications of Strategic Thinking in Multi-National Companies

Articulating an organization's direction is where *strategic thinking* begins. Where it continues, as a thought process, is in the minds of executives who share a common direction through consensus.

Clients have used *strategic thinking* to reorganize, consolidate, divest, acquire, and change market attitude and direction. The following case studies represent a cross-section of clients who have used the process with great success. Again, confidentiality precludes us from identifying them.

FORTUNE 50 MULTI-PRODUCT CORPORATION

It has been explained how a multi-product company can have a hierarchy of driving forces. That is the case with a major U.S. multi-division client, obviously technology-driven as a corporation, yet product-driven or user/market–driven within selected divisions and subsidiaries. One division was found to have two driving forces, split by market—a technology orientation on the domestic front, and product-driven overseas. This "split personality" led to a lot of disagreements over product and market priorities.

Strategic thinking has allowed the division to rank its activities in priority. To that end, it is using the process to plan its worldwide strategic priorities for process control development, quality control, and product engineering.

This division perceives the process as an ongoing strategic tool, as the division vice-president comments: "The process does not stop, but continues as an established thinking and planning process that has further complemented the operational matrix."

The same executive differentiates between the operational matrix and its planning system, and *strategic thinking* and its potential for change: "For planning the future, *strategic thinking* is a superior process to operational planning. The latter starts at the top and works its way down. The former starts at the bottom and works its way up. Thus, operational planning does nothing to change the nature or direction of a company because top executives aren't involved until the end."

Coordinates Subsidiary Activities

Within the same corporation, another division used the process to coordinate the activities of its three separate sites, and change hiring needs and direction. "There was a need for a certain consolidation of group think," says the general manager. "The process got all the managers to think as one group for the first time and to think strategically for a change. They had always thought about their own specializations rather than think on a group basis."

The group's realization of its *driving force* also dictated hiring practices. "Most people recognized they were driven by technology," he says. "Others weren't comfortable with that conclusion. A few, in retrospect, left the organization out of their own volition when they realized they were not in tune with the technological bias of the group."

Given that the subsidiary was technology-driven dictated the type and caliber of staff needed to support the *driving force* and business concept of the organization. It gave the group direction on where to allocate resources and made those decisions easier, he says.

For this executive, one word expresses the benefits he and the organization realized from the DPI sessions: crystallization. "Without crystallization, it looks like management directly from above. People who didn't know each other got to know the mind-set of the group and consensus was achieved."

Transcends Numbers Orientation

When the corporation was restructured three years ago, three formerly independent units became one division. Naturally, it was essential to form a cohesive management team.

"Not only did we form a team, but we did it with a common understanding of division direction and objectives through real consensus," says yet another division vice-president. "Thus, the strategic profile of our business, which we have been using as a guide ever since, was the product of the management team."

The same executive found the process as transcending the numbers orientation of operational planning.

"The process expands thinking to more than just a series of number projections. It offers a strategic profile to use on an ongoing basis. The key component of this plan is the *driving force*, or source of company momentum, which, in our case, is market type."

"The combination of the corporate plan and strategic profile enhances overall planning by adding a sense of company identity and direction to the number projections," he says. "By being identified as market-driven, we are more aware of the needs of the marketplace as the technology changes. This has put us in a position to design better products to meet specific needs."

For still another division, the notion of being market-driven has moved it in the right direction.

"At least four new products are being tested and four are on the drawing board," says the division vice-president. "We can attribute that to the concentrated effort brought on by *strategic thinking* which has supplied divisional management with a language with which we can communicate."

"The process is very effective with material effect on our volume and profit. It has helped us restructure the company, separate "good" from "good" as well as "good" from "bad" opportunities, make better decisions, and keep our collective and individual eyes on the correct priorities," he points out. "My team has a better perspective of where we are going. The critical issues are still on the agenda at our monthly management committee meetings, reflecting our on-going commitment."

In still another unit of this corporation, there was a subsidiary which had always been a business operating in a reactive mode. This attitude was changed as a result of employing DPI's *strategic thinking* process. For the general manager, it was a welcome relief.

"We were being driven by survival and the whims of the market. We needed a third party to help us sort out our identity direction and driving force. I felt *strategic thinking* and its DPI facilitator would work well for a small high-tech company."

"We thought we were technology-driven. After a lot of discussion, however, we came to the conclusion that we were product-driven, and it surprised quite a few people."

"A product-driven organization survives on the quality and performance of its products. As a result, product development has become a new and critical emphasis area and has set the mood for resource allocation and market segment identification."

Strategic Profile

For each *driving force* there is a business concept or basic idea that perpetuates an organization. For this subsidiary, the business concept expanded into a strategic profile, defined its identity, and laid the foundation for the firm's new direction.

"We had formerly viewed ourselves as the resource for all comers," this general manager points out, "and had expended a lot of energy on non-productive opportunities. Now we represent ourselves as a product-oriented electronic OEM-dominated image processing company."

"In formulating the strategic profile, the process helped us realize why failures and successes had occurred and it built up people's confidence. Now that we know what we do well, we can dabble in new markets where our products might be appropriate."

Critical Issues

A set of critical issues has simplified resource allocation and decision making.

"Using the critical issues as a guideline, we have proceeded to invest in the technical personnel and capital equipment facilities we need."

"Reviewing the critical issues makes decision-making simple in placing emphasis on new business development. Since the process, we have honed in to very specific product market segments and are aggressively pursuing those segments."

Overall Perspective

Perhaps the best summary of why this corporation decided to use our *strategic thinking* process and cascade its use down into many of the divisions and subsidiaries is best stated by one of the group vice-presidents.

"We've done five-year planning and annual planning," he says. "But that was all primarily operational and financial planning for the company. Our sector needed strategic direction. Since it is composed of groups and divisions headed by managers with divergent views, we didn't know where to start."

"When we began to put a plan together, we tried to do so without a process," he says. "We needed a centerpiece, a peg. That peg was the *driving force* in DPI's process. The driving force was the glue that brought us all together."

"We discovered where he had commonality, where we had leverage, and exactly who our competition was."

Through DPI, the sector identified areas of emphasis and de-emphasis resulting in a significant divestiture and a shift in priorities. "We have quite a few splinter businesses and when you have businesses that don't follow your strategic profile, you must recognize them for what they are. If we're going to make a change or consider an acquisition, now we can test it against our strategic profile. It's a uniform strategy, a plan used by all. It acts as the motive to keep everyone on the corporate level talking the same language."

In the past two years our process has been used by twenty-two of this corporation's business units and the above stories are just a few of the many that could have been reprinted here. To attempt to tell each of the twenty-two stories to date could be enough material for a book in itself.

FROM DIVISION TO SUBSIDIARY

Our client, one of the world's largest ferry companies, rose from annual operating losses of $3 million in 1981 to a $10 million profit in 1983 after a technical and corporate restructuring and a emphasis on *strategic thinking*.

When the new managing director took the helm of this company, it had just merged with its major competitor. The new CEO, who had been called in from the parent company to manage the new ferry entity, quickly realized that it was not enough to reorganize the ferry company's technical structure.

"The line needed to generate more revenue," he says. "The management at the parent company had ordered two jumbo luxury ferries at $50 million each in 1978 for delivery in 1983. The cost was substantially higher than the other vessels that had been purchased for about $3 million each. Since the management made money by selling the vessels, not by operating them, they had not anticipated the effect of additional operating losses on the line."

The firm's operations manager adds,

"The management had always thought in terms of short-range profit. They were efficient at day-to-day operational concerns, not strategy. The did not forecast beyond the budget year."

Management Attitude

The market for European ferries, considered the best built in the world, is excellent. Vessels bought for $2-3 million from the shipyard fetch $50 million five years later in other parts of the continent.

"It is easy to understand the attitude of the owners," he says. "The operation was viewed as storage for the vessels until they were sold. The cheaper the storage, the better. Employees were considered a cost."

"We wanted to make the operation profitable," he adds. "In fact, we had to. Two to three years down the channel, we would not have been able to cover the cost of the new vessels. But it was also a matter of pride. It is not so satisfying for the company to make a profit from one or two managers who sell a vessel every year. It is certainly not the best thing for 2,000 employees. We wanted the profit to come from the personnel."

The obstacles to raising revenues included overcapacity—which the merger was designed to eliminate—artificially low fares during the off-season, and traditionally poor service with two luxury vessels on their way.

Transportation Outfit

Since 1962, this ferry line had operated as a transportation business carrying trucks, freight, passengers, and cars. During the summer, a busy tourist season filled the vessels. Onboard, passengers dined, drank, and purchased tax-free goods, primarily perfume, cigarettes, chocolate, and wine, during the three to fourteen-hour runs.

But in the off-season, from September to May, revenues depended more on conference services and truck transport than tourists. To attract more passengers, fares were held artificially low. Despite bargain fares, however, both lines suffered operating losses from overcapacity.

"Every morning at 8 o'clock, our vessels would start out, as would our competitor's, from the same point, half empty," the CEO says. "Since the people were travelling practically free, there was no motivation to provide good service. You can't expect something for free, especially from employees who work the 14-hour run five days a week."

From an operating standpoint he and his team cut overcapacity by limiting the number of outgoing vessels from six to three. Other savings resulted from cuts in personnel and overhead.

"We have always been an efficient company with high technical standards," he says. "That was not a problem. The problem was that operating changes did not raise revenue. We did not like giving 'free tickets' to half of our passengers each year. We wanted them to pay. But we knew they wouldn't pay a higher fare on a luxury ferry if they didn't get service."

"So, we needed another concept or business idea. We needed to change the management and the employees both on paper and inside the people themselves. We weren't sure how to go about that."

Strategic Thinking Process

The CEO had met the author of this book at a *strategic thinking* project at another firm. He saw the DPI process as a means of getting his management team and the parent company's top management to discuss strategy, something that had never been done before.

The process involved ten people. Of the many changes agreed to, the best result of the discussions was the discussions was the full support of the company's owners. "It was important to have the owners' approval since what we discussed was not a surface change, but some very deep changes."

According to the CEO, *strategic thinking* reinforced some common beliefs about the company and also pointed out internal changes and external potential threats. There was no question, for example, that the ferry line was capacity-driven and had efficiency and aggressive marketing as its strengths. The internal changes, on the other hand, were dramatic. The ferry line was separated from the parent company and made a subsidiary. It now leases ferries from the parent. "We needed to create our own culture separate from the big, tough, conglomerate managers," he points out.

Another major change was making each terminal a profit center with its own marketing, catering, and freight departments instead of having one marketing or catering department for all five terminals. "This made a lot of sense," he says, "since each line serves a different market with its own type of passenger, prices, trip duration, and destination. Now the main advantage of each line is marketed."

Employee Motivation

By operating separately from the parent company, the company has succeeded in motivating its employees to serve people instead of just transporting them. In fact, the entire business concept has changed—from the transport and tax-free company to a travel services company.

In adhering to the new business concept, they closed down a video company and a charter bus operation because they did not fit into a capacity-driven ferry-based travel service orientation.

"It was all a shock at first," says the operation manager, "and many employees were resistant to the changes. After all, we changed the culture and the objectives. Different people were required. Some of the employees we had no longer fit. This is one of the critical issues we'll be working on for the next two to three years."

"The highlight is now on quality service and we have a better image in the marketplace because of it," the CEO says. "We are no longer a storage medium. Now we develop products to fit leisure needs and we're realizing a five percent increase in market share per year. Again, this had never been done before. The company always filled internal needs first. There is a trend toward more frequent, closer, and shorter voyages and we're filling that need. Our prices are still cheap compared to a trip to the Mediterranean, so we're competing favorably with other travel service companies."

Among the threats fleshed out by the sessions was the possibility of the government stopping onboard tax-free sales (one-third of company gross income), and the railway's new piggyback service that could cut into the ferry's truck transport business.

"Now at least we're aware of threats to the business and the needs of the market," he says. "We're also learned that operational skills are not enough. You also have to know how to motivate your people to work the right way. The ships are only the ticket into the market. Our success is based on how we perform. It was a tough job to make the owners understand our vision of the company and our different perspective of looking at the personnel. Strategic thinking has taken us this far, but we still have much to do."

BIO-MEDICAL TECHNOLOGY COMPANY DIVISION

When a division of a major medical technology company was formed in 1981, the vice-president/general manager had two objectives.

First, he needed to focus management's attention on the division's major business, a $40 million market that had not been sufficiently addressed. Second, he wanted to diversify the company's unique technical and manufacturing capabilities.

"When we looked at potential product and business areas for diversification,"he says, "we developed a list of 20 product areas that our technology could develop. When it came time to decide on one of these areas, however, we lacked a process that would help us narrow the range of opportunities."

"The *strategic thinking* process succeeded in providing the framework the six-member management team needed. The process resulted in a strategic profile that identified the new business area, a list of critical issues to resolve, a driving force describing the division's impetus and a working consensus to implement the plan."

The *driving force*, the general manager notes, defined the division's basic objectives, strengths and weaknesses, and areas of reinforcement and importance.

"Before the concept was introduced, different managers had thought we were market-driven, technology-driven, or product-driven. In retrospect it seems clear that we were technology-driven. But it wasn't clear at the time we held this discussion."

Driving force was just one part of the precise terminology the process provided the group with which to expedite the discussion.

"We had been limiting ourselves to one or two potential segments," he says. "In articulating a strategic profile, the discussion was broadened to a more general business approach. We considered the entire area of critical care monitoring and decided we would expand in that area. It has turned out to be a very good decision, even more attractive now, nearly two years later."

The management team has since used the strategic profile as a filter for decisions. It has also proved to be an excellent means of reaching group consensus. "Without this structure and format, we might have spent a year talking about diversification without ever reaching a consensus. Having everyone's commitment is very important to the success of a project."

With consensus and a direction, the division was better able to allocate resources. "We have put all our resources into critical care monitoring and have terminated a number of projects we had been expending money and energy on. Since it takes two years to develop products in a heavily regulated market, a framework for decision making and planning is crucial. *Strategic thinking* has directly influenced the division's development of two innovative products for future release."

STRATEGIC IMPOTENCE IN THE POWER INDUSTRY

The managing director of one of Europe's largest multi-nationals did not like what was happening. The corporate planning offices had too much influence in his company. The strategic plans produced by these department had often proved too quantitative and unwieldy for successful implementation. Operating managers, excluded from the strategy planning process, had often shelved the formula-matrix approaches passed along to them. When formula plans were followed, a reliance on data instead of market instinct led to bad strategies and spotty results.

In an effort to reduce data and increase thinking, this chief executive wanted a strategy based on implementation through consensus. DPI's approach was to his liking because it placed emphasis on thinking rather than matrices.

The major business of this company is the manufacture of turbines for nuclear power plants. The company also produces conventional equipment for power electronics and automation, and supplies customers worldwide. Its customers are users of sophisticated power electronic equipment who have their own production facilities. The company is also working with contractors for projects throughout the British Commonwealth and the Middle East.

The group must be able to manage many fields of activities: from component sales to systems sales, from a turbine to a piece of cable, from a highly sophisticated electronic sensing device to a high voltage switch gear. Some of these activities are more important than others. Knowing which to emphasize at a certain time requires strategy. According to the CEO, developing a strategy should not be done in isolation.

Developing a Strategy

"For a manager to plot a strategy and present it to his people is a lonely experience," he says. "He is the only one who believes in the plan, and he ends up working alone to accomplish it. For an outside planner who is not involved in the day-to-day operation, it is even worse. If you get your people involved in the process so that it becomes their strategy developed together with you, your chances of success are greater."

Most managers, he observes, are so preoccupied with operational concerns they don't even plot a strategy.

"They don't look outside their current operational involvement. They look beyond it, they must step aside, put themselves above what they're doing, and look at it. For that, you need a structured format, a strategy session. Otherwise, you reinvent the wheel."

"The key to strategic thinking is the *driving force*," he says. "The *driving force* propels a company in a certain direction. If you know what your *driving force* is and relate your product lines to that driving force, you will be able to develop a strategy. If you don't understand your driving force, you may wind up allocating resources for a fringe activity. To make decisions for the future I must know where I'm going and what I now hold in my hand. Strategic thinking helps chart that direction."

A Product/Services—Driven Company

The company determined that it was product/services-driven and formulated a strategy and list of areas of emphasis to support that *driving force*. The CEO feels that the statement of corporate strategy has determined what the management should do in the future. The statement is important to articulate to the rest of the staff.

The key to profitability, the managers found, is for the company to produce high quality products and maintain a tireless drive for technical excellence. The firm will succeed by providing services for the distribution of energy and be universally recognized as being above average in quality and reliability. Systems engineering must be of the highest quality, The company must exploit the market potential of the United Kingdom, and then expand worldwide. It must also develop a close working relationship with its head office colleagues in maintaining a high quality engineering staff.

The areas of emphasis which the team decided upon include: putting together an automation systems team, developing and hiring expertise in the United Kingdom so that the subsidiary would no longer be completely dependent on its corporate parent, and to emphasize new, high-tech products, and de-emphasize old, conventional equipment.

The team also examined its past performance as a company and the success or lack of success of the parent company. "We determined the winners over there to see if we could succeed with them in the UK. We searched for a combined excellence," he says.

The process has proved invaluable, says the CEO. Not only does the company continue to be profitable, but the strategy is still being followed two years later. "In the next half year we're going to have another DPI session to see what changes we should make, if any."

CONFUSION IN THE RANKS

Another of America's top-rated companies used DPI's process for a very specific reason. A maker and marketer of building controls equipment, it had reached a point where its strategic direction was unclear.

"We had no real idea of where we were going as a company," says the chief executive. "We made small profits despite ourselves." The vice-president agreed. "We were making money but we had no direction."

After bringing the top eighteen executives together through the *strategic thinking* process, these same two executives were interviewed some fourteen months later.

"I liked the methodical, no-nonsense approach of extracting key ideas and thoughts in a non-threatening manner," cites the chief executive. "The process is simple and understandable and breeds agreement and commitment."

"Our ability to communicate our purpose to all members of management," adds the vice-president, "and a shared commitment set the table for developing effective action plans to satisfy the critical issues. The strategic profile gives us a tool to measure opportunities against a plan for fit, not for a chance at making money."

"In the last nine months, we have had the fastest and most successful new product introduction in the company's history. The new product introduction cycle used to be three years. We did it in nine months because everyone understood their role and was committed to the project," he adds. "We've come a long way in a short time," concurs the CEO.

FOURTEEN

Applications of Strategic Thinking in Owner-Managed Companies

ANIMAL NUTRITION COMPANY

A client's ability to market animal feed and analyze forages helped build it into a major animal nutrition company. The dairy farmer supplier used *strategic thinking* to articulate and clarify its identity and market emphasis.

"Up until a year ago, we were going in 10 different directions," says the company owner/president. "We were aware of it, but never addressed the problem. We never stopped to ask ourselves whether we should allocate resources and develop expertise in specific market areas."

When a member of the board of directors asked him where the company would be in five years, he said he expected sales to be $80 million primarily generated from dairy producers. "It was a typical response from a financial person," he says. "What he really wanted to know was what the company was going to look like and how it was going to serve its markets. We hadn't thought of that and didn't know how to address the issue."

Direction and Consensus

"The facilitator was a great asset," he says. "It would be very difficult for a person inside the company to lead a similar discussion because of personal prejudice or lack of skill."

"'As for the process, it gave everyone an opportunity to voice their ideas on various activities and markets. This was invaluable. Between what they thought the company was and what they thought I wanted it to be, we had quite a diversity of opinion."

Through the formalized discussion, that diversity of opinion was transformed into general consensus. A strategic profile and list of critical issues were drawn in support of the driving force and business concept geared to satisfying customer needs, and the result was a tremendous transition for the company.

Not Just a Feed Company

"The profile has definitely clarified our markets," he says. "We were saying that we were a feed company or a dairy company serving our dealers. Our profile states that we are truly an animal nutrition company serving dairy producers. This notion has steered us away from non-dairy markets which has been a hell of a break for us."

The company markets animal feed and preservatives nationwide. The company also offers on-farm technical support such as nutritional analysis to help farmers obtain the highest possible payback on feed costs while meeting requirements for milk and egg production.

"The strategic profile has helped us tie our preservatives business with our animal nutrition business, clarify our market position in New York and California, strengthen our service activities and increase direct work with the customer," he points out. "We use this profile on a day-to-day basis to assign manhours and allocate other resources in the proper areas. it has also helped us to de-emphasize other non-dairy product lines such as chicken, hog and pet foods."

The critical issues are evaluated during the company's regularly scheduled meetings and the company expects to update and replace them according to changes in the business.

EDUCATIONAL SPECIALTIES FIRM

The client, which markets a variety of stickers, mini-books, four-color cartoon newsgrams, certificates, and pencil toppers to preschool and grade school children, doubled its sales in 1982, the result of product development and distribution outside its traditional school market. Such phenomenal growth, however, found the company's president overwhelmed with operational details, leaving little time to plot the company's future direction.

The president/owner explains,

"Five years ago, we distributed our products solely through educational channels such as school supply stores. We had always concentrated on the school market where products, such as scratch'n sniff stick-ons denoting the appearance and fragrance of an orange, for example, are used as resource guides. We were reluctant to explore retail outlets because when children have access to our products at home, we found they won't use them at school."

A great consumer demand, however, prompted the firm to develop different products for sale in toy stores, supermarkets, and gift stationery shops.

"Our sales began increasing 40 percent a year, all supervised by an informal organizational structure," she says. "I didn't know what doubling sales would mean, but we were having a hard enough time keeping up with the operation to do any kind of planning. I realized it was time to reorganize and we sought out an outside consultant. We chose Decision Processes International because their process, *strategic thinking*, required the active involvement of our own people."

The main problem, which the process addressed, concerned the company's split into retail and education divisions. "We had a great deal of operational problems because we had two separate sets of elements— marketing, accounting, distribution and production—going on simultaneously," she explains. "*Strategic thinking* helped us form a strategic profile which has redefined the company and set a direction for us to follow."

Consolidation and Market Direction

As a result of the process, the company has combined the two divisions and now uses multiple distribution channels. The company has used the strategic profile to identify other market segments and to begin distribution overseas. "The profile states that our organization will always design products characterized by their education and play value for parents, teachers and children," the president says. "By knowing exactly what our business is, we have been better able to investigate a vast untapped market potential."

The profile has also led the president's nine-member management team to reshuffle priorities and allocate resources in the product development area. Pricing structures and sales policies have also been redrawn.

"Our discussion of *driving force* proved to us that we had started as a product-driven company but are now driven by user needs," the president says. "Naturally, that has changed our focus. Suddenly we realized that we would have to develop innovative products and be a leader in our field, not a follower. We had been reactive. Now we're proactive."

"We use this profile on a day-to-day basis," the chief executive adds. "It acts as an easy screening device or filter for all our decisions."

Aside from defining a company's business concept and reaffirming its products and markets, *strategic thinking* also achieves consensus among the members of the management team, certainly a critical factor to the success of the chosen direction.

Framework for Discussion

As the company has grown, the amount of personal attention has diminished. Thus, the firm needed to identify an organizational structure in which every member would feel important. "We had a large group of independent thinkers and no order in which to proceed." the president points out. "With *strategic thinking* we know to what extent people would be involved in a project. Also, everyone is aware of the company's new direction and what is required to pursue that direction."

When it came to choosing that order, the executive mentions that— unlike the long- and short-range planning offered by most consultancy services—DPI's *strategic thinking* was a process that enabled a company to discuss and formulate a strategy and direction by itself with the help of an outside facilitator.

"The long- and short-range planning didn't work for us," the president says. "Our problems were much more complex than any textbook approach. We needed a road map. We had worked through all the manuals and it was time for some clarity. Finally, we found a process that worked."

A MAJOR CONSUMER MAGAZINE PUBLISHING COMPANY

A successful magazine publishing company can diversify in a number of areas. It can delve into related media such as cable TV, establish business sidelines, expand its publication rosters, or focus its resources on its flagship title. This was the crossroads the chairman and staff of a major consumer magazine for women faced in 1983.

When the present chairman joined the company, he found his staff pursuing ventures that, while related to the interests of the magazine audience, would diffuse the strength of the publication in the long run.

Too Many Opportunities, Not Enough Focus

"There were a variety of business offshoots in the works that were seeking to exploit the name: seminars, umbrellas, T-shirts, all kinds of licensing deals," he explains. "These activities had definite profit potential. They weren't bad. They were just happening without any real plan."

He though it better to concentrate the same energies into maximizing the magazine. "We had a hot property, but also one that could easily and quickly be pre-empted by one of the giant publishers through heavy expenditures in circulation and editorial."

"I could have dictated to the staff what I wanted to do, but it's a whole lot better if they reach the conclusion themselves. In that way, they're working their plan and know how and why they chose it. That's where DPI came in."

The process helped the 10-member management team determine the magazine's current and future position in the magazine industry. Among other topics discussed were the future role of magazines in the media mix, the company's strengths and weaknesses and those of its competitors, and the nature and future of its business.

In the magazine industry, there were many paths to consider. Following the Ziff-Davis tradition, for example, would involve an accumulation of special interest titles produced by separate staffs. Other options included concentrating on a single title, a success formula exhibited by *U.S. News & World Report* and perhaps to be continued under its new ownership, or expanding demographics and titles to pursue a Conde Nast type audience.

Different Views of the Business

In addition to direction, there was the question of defining the business itself.

"Depending on who you talked to, you would get a different definition of our purpose," says the general manager of outside ventures. "Ask someone in advertising and they would say the magazine was a medium for carrying an advertiser's message. Ask an editorial person and she would likely say we're in the business of providing products and services to a defined set of customers in the American marketplace."

The company decided it was in the business of publishing a unique monthly magazine with supporting services and products to an upscale female professional/managerial audience. The majority of company resources would be allocated toward this business concept. The staff would only pursue ancillary projects if they would strengthen and enhance the magazine's demographics, image, editorial quality, and size. The projects would not act as profit centers and would be self-liquidating, if possible.

Concept of Driving Force

The key behind these conclusions lay with the company's *driving force*.

"Everyone had a different idea about the driving force," the general manager recalls. "Since I had been hired to develop products and services for our market segments, I thought we were market-driven."

"After the discussion, however, it was clear that we could not afford to be driven by the market. We were, in fact, product-driven and there was absolute consensus on that point," the manager notes.

By the end of the process, the executive thought she was out of a job. Actually, her job had changed. "I had to realize that I was still in magazine publishing," she says, "and that I had to think constantly about the product."

She now uses three criteria to evaluate deals with outside companies: every project undertaken must enhance the image of the magazine or at least be consistent with the editorial premise; no project can compete with the magazine's advertising revenue stream; and projects must be profitable.

New Perspective

Since the magazine must be sensitive to advertising budgets and be responsive to an always visible competition, the general manager and her staff deal with a seven-year timeframe when considering projects.

"I no longer develop products," she says. "I develop services. I keep in mind that we're not expert in everything. When we got into book publishing, for example, we didn't write and sell the book ourselves. We sold the idea to a book publisher. When we established a speakers' bureau, we set policy and described the financial structure of the deal, but hired an outside company to operate it. Without the benefit of *strategic thinking*, we would have been in certain businesses instead of being part of them. That's what driving force did for us."

"I think we caught the problem at the right time, when we were just on the verge of going astray," the chairman says. "Now we have a master plan, a strategic profile. As things come up, we compare them to this profile. Now the staff feels they have a say in the direction of the company. Everyone speaks the same language and understands that direction. Right away you avoid the long debates."

The general manager believes that the DPI process got department heads to think about the interrelationships of their activities and the effects of their decisions on the other departments.

"DPI's process gets you thinking about implementation and avoids the analysis paralysis," she adds. "It provides you with a framework upon which to base future decisions."

FUZZY VISION IN A HIGHLY SUCCESSFUL COMPANY?

The following client organization is a fast-growing and highly successful manufacturer of pressure-sensitive laminated material sold to a variety of end-users primarily through printers. This company, we predict, will be a billion-dollar company within the next seven to ten years. It is currently a $120 million organization and growing at a rate of over 25% per year. It is competing against some of the largest and "best managed" American and Japanese companies and . . . *winning*! Why would the CEO, evidently a good strategist already, want to use DPI's strategic thinking process in view of his organization's outstanding track record? He explains it this way,

"Six or seven years ago, three or four of us could get into a room for a few hours and agree on what the strategy was and how to implement it," he says. "Then we would leave and carry it out. Today, with 750 people, that is no longer possible."

The chief operating officer adds these thoughts:

"We were highly profitable, growing rapidly with many motivated and dedicated people. However, some of the growth was chaotic with many people pulling in different directions. We wanted to bring our key executives together to agree on a direction, a common purpose, our company philosophy and to set a strategy to meet the challenges of our next growth cycle."

The first three-day retreat was scheduled and involved the top twenty-three executives of the firm. Although this was a slightly larger number of people than are usually involved, it was felt that growth had brought with it a need to promote people to senior positions more quickly and the CEO felt that these people should show a common vision as quickly as possible.

"What surprised me," said the CEO later, "was DPI's ability to keep the process on track while involving every person in it. Everyone's opinion was heard and several times some of these opinions actually helped me change my mind about certain issues."

"This kind of a process is impossible to accomplish without an outside facilitator," adds the COO. "Although there are several structured assignments, the facilitator is the one that keeps the discussion objective and on target. We had attempted to do this before without a process as a framework and we got nowhere. We might still be there if we had not come in contact with DPI's process."

The vice-president of marketing had these additional comments to offer.

"I've seen a remarkable improvement in our teamwork. There is now much cohesiveness among cross-functional groups who are working on some of the critical issues. They are now all working towards the same goals. Exploring different driving forces and the scenarios of where each would lead us gave us a chance to explore the implications of each scenario. We quickly realized we could not be market-driven as we had thought before going into the process. Recognizing that we were technology-driven helped us prioritize our product development program much more clearly. We have since de-emphasized commodity products and re-emphasized more promising new technology-based programs."

As the company had grown over the years, it had opened a European subsidiary. Originally, it had done so primarily at the request of clients who wanted some material to use there. Over the years, the company has somewhat reluctantly built a small organization to service this business. However, there was perpetual conflict between this small European operation and the corporate office in the United States over product development priorities, manpower, expertise, and customer service. DPI was called in to do a "mini" strategy session with the COO and the key managers in Europe in an attempt "to straighten them out over there," as the COO put it.

"The European session was probably of even greater value to us than the corporate one," he now says. "We had some very frank exchanges and my entire perspective as to how we should conduct our business in Europe changed during this session even though we had made several attempts, without a process, however, to deal with this issue before. The session resulted in a complete change of our USA sales policy of not calling on end-users. The environmental analysis we did convinced me that the way of doing business was different and a different approach was needed. 'Since then our business has boomed. They straightened me out.'"

Bibliography

PUBLICATIONS

American Way
   "What Motivates Mary Kay" (October 1984).

B.C. Business
   "The Third Leg Strategy" (December 1981).

Business Week
   "How D&B Organizes for a New Product Blitz" (November 1981).
   "How Sir Freddie Shot Himself Down" (February 1982).
   "The Consumer Drives R. J. Reynolds Again" (June 1984).
   "Alcan Goes Toe to Toe With Alcoa" (August 1984).
   "High Fashion Arrives at 'Fuddy-Duddy, Old Inflexible Burlington' " (August
      1984).
   "The Perils in Financial Services" (August 1984).
   "The New Breed of Strategic Planner" (September 1984).
   "Shaklee: Sweetening Incentives to Spur Its Sales Force" (September 1984).
   "A Bolder Timken Streamlines Its Steel Plants to Finesse Tough Markets" (Oc-
      tober 1984).
   "Champion Struggles to Make the St. Regis Merger Work" (February 1985).
   "The Toughest Job in Business" (February 1985).
   "A Troubled Polaroid is Tearing Down the House That Land Built" (April
      1985).

"Do Mergers Really Work" (June 1985).
"Behind the AMF Takeover" (August 1985).
"The Third World's Growth Crisis" (August 1985).
"Texas Instruments Cleans Up Its Act" (September 1985).
"Digital Equipment: A Step Ahead in Linking Computers" (April 1986).
"IBM: Trying to Put All the Pieces Together" (April 1986).
"How Olivetti Cloned Its Way to the Top" (June 1986).
"Inside the Troubled Empire of Peter Grace" (June 1986).
"What's Causing the Scratches in Dupont's Teflon" (December 1986).
"The IBM–DEC Wars: The Year of the Customer" (March 1987).

Dun's Business Month
"3M's Unusual Strategy" (April 1983).

ERA
"Seizing the Moment" (June 1984).

Excellence
"Avon Calling . . . What's New in Management" (October 1985).

Forbes
"Import Quotas: The Honda Dealer's Best Friend" (December 1983).
"Good-bye Animal House" (November 1984).
"Like the Kid at F.A.O.Schwarz" (May 1985).
"Interview with A. Hammer" (June 1985).
"The Antique Shop in Athol" (November 1985).
"Best Car Wins" (January 1986).
"It's Time to Take Risks" (October 1986).
"Store for Our Times" (November 1986).
"Use a Long Spoon" (December 1986).
"What Makes a Survivor" (January 1987).
"The Vindication of Edwin Land" (May 1987).

Fortune
"J&J Comes a Long Way from Baby" (June 1981).
"Corporate Strategists Under Fire" (December 1982).
"Allegheny Ludlum Has Steel Figured Out" (June 1984).
"Breaking Out of a Niche Can Hurt" (July 1984).
"Exxon Rededicates Itself to Oil and Gas" (July 1984).
"Merrill Lynch's Not-So-Thundering Recovery Plan" (August 1984).
"Fare Wars: Have the Big Airlines Learned to Win?" (October 1984).
"McDonald's Refuses to Plateau" (November 1984).
"Why Harry Gray Can't Let Go at United Technologies" (November 1984).
"Behind the Fall of Steve Jobs" (August 1985).
"Scott Isn't Lumbering Any More" (September 1985).
"America's New No. 4 Automaker—Honda" (October 1985).
"Pioneer Hi-Bred's Crop of Profits" (October 1985).
"How to Make Money in Mature Markets" (November 1985).
"Volkswagen Regains Some Beetle Margin" (March 1986).
"How We Rebuilt Jaguar in the U.S." (April 1986).
"Merck Has Made Biotech Work" (January 1987).

Harvard Business Review
"Planning on the Right Side, Managing on the Left" (February 1980).

Inc.
"Excellence in Medium-Sized Companies" (December 1983).
"That Daring Young Man and His Flying Machines" (January 1984).
"Murphy's Law" (July 1984).

Insight
"Auto Industry's Power That Was" (November 1986).

International Business
"Interview with Masaru Ikuba" (January 1982).

International Management
"Voices & Views" (October 1984).

Journal of Business Strategy
"The Failure of Business Planning" (March 1986).

Planning Review
"Fortune 500 Dropouts" (May 1986).

Scandinavian Business World
"Profile of Holck Andersen" (January 1982).

Time
"D-Day for the Home Computer" (November 1983).
"Slimmed Way Down and Styled Up" (November 1986).

U.S. News & World Report
"Effective Leadership: The Exception, Not the Rule" (April 1983).
"When a New Breed of Bosses Takes Over" (February 1984).

Venture
"How Entrepreneurs Maintain Their Imprint" (May 1982).
"Lessons Learned When Blue Chips Fail" (May 1982).
"Publishers Shift to Small Presses" (June 1983).

World Business
"British Companies Plan by Hunch" (May 1983).

BOOKS

Brant, Steven C. *Strategic Planning in Emerging Companies*. Menlo Park, Calif.:
    Addison-Wesley, 1981.
Clifford, Donald K., Jr., and Richard E. Cavanagh. *The Winning Performance:
    How America's High-Growth Midsize Companies Survive*. New York: Ban-
    tam Books, 1985.
Drucker, Peter F. *Innovation and Entrepreneurship: Practice and Principles*. New
    York: Harper and Row, 1985.
Guth, William D. *Handbook of Business Strategy*, 3 vols. Boston: Warren, Gorham
    & Lamont, 1985, 1986, 1987.

Hamermesh, Richard. *Making Strategy Work: How Senior Managers Produce Results*. New York: John Wiley & Sons, 1986.

Harvard Business Review. *Strategic Management*. New York: John Wiley & Sons, 1983.

Henderson, Carter. *Winners: The Successful Strategies Entrepreneurs Use to Build New Businesses*. New York: Holt, Rinehart and Winston, 1985.

Kotler, Philip, William Fahey, and S. Jatusripitak. *The New Competition*. Englewood Cliffs, N.J.: Prentice-Hall, 1985.

Morita, Akio et al. *Made in Japan: Akio Morita and the Sony Corporation*. Edited by Jennifer Josephy. New York: E.P. Dutton, 1986.

Porter, Michael. *Competitive Advantage: Creating and Sustaining Superior Performance*. New York: Free Press, 1985.

———. *Competitive Strategy: Techniques for Analyzing Industries and Competitors*. New York: Free Press, 1980.

Rich, Stanley R., and David Gumpert. *Business Plans That Win Dollars: Lessons from the MIT Enterprise Forum*. New York: Harper and Row, 1985.

Ries, Al, and Jack Trout. *Marketing Warfare*. New York: NAL, Plume Books, 1986.

Rothschild, William E. *Putting It All Together: A Guide to Strategic Thinking*. New York: AMACOM, 1986.

Shanklin, William L., and John K. Ryans, Jr. *Thinking Strategically*. New York: Random House, 1985.

Sloan, Alfred P., Jr. *My Years with General Motors*. Edited by John McDonald and Catherine Stevens. New York: Doubleday, 1972.

Waddell, William C. *The Outline of Strategy*. Oxford, Ohio: Planning Forum, 1986.

Index

About the Author

MICHEL ROBERT received his Bachelor in Commerce from Concordia University in Montreal, and is a founding partner of Decision Processes International (DPI), which has 60 partners in 15 countries and aids in improving their strategic and operational decisions. He served in senior management positions with several major corporations such as Johnson & Johnson, Nabisco Brands, and Smith, Kline and Beckman before founding Decision Processes International. He lives in Westport, Connecticut, where the company (DPI) is headquartered.